A Practical Reader in
Universal Design for Learning

A Practical Reader in Universal Design for Learning

Edited by

DAVID H. ROSE *and* ANNE MEYER

Center for Applied Special Technology (CAST)

HARVARD EDUCATION PRESS

Cambridge, Massachusetts

Library of Congress Control Number 2006930073

Paperback ISBN 1-891792-29-6
Library Edition ISBN 1-891792-30-X

13-Digit Paperback ISBN 978-1-891792-29-8
13-Digit Library Edition ISBN 978-1-891792-30-4

Published by Harvard Education Press,
an imprint of the Harvard Education Publishing Group

Harvard Education Press
8 Story Street
Cambridge, MA 02138

Cover Design: Anne Carter

The typefaces used in this book are Sabon for text and Myriad for display.
.

Contents

Preface

ANNE MEYER AND DAVID H. ROSE

Sometimes a simple shift in perspective can change not only how we see the world but how we live in it. In 1958, electrical engineer Jack S. Kilby questioned standard thinking in his industry by suggesting that both active electronic components (transistors) and passive ones (resistors and capacitors) could be made from the same semiconductor material and linked together at the point of manufacture. This eliminated the need for soldering many parts together in bulky modules. Kilby's brainstorm led to the creation of the integrated circuit, or microchip, which in turn ushered in the digital computer age. Think of the extraordinary changes in manufacturing, media, transportation, medicine, education, business, and entertainment brought about by Kilby's simple *what if?*

What if? also lies at the core of Universal Design for Learning (UDL). What if all learners had genuine opportunities to learn in inclusive environments? What if we recognized that our inflexible curricula and learning environments are "disabled" rather than pinning that label on learners who face unnecessary barriers? Beginning in the 1980s, we and our colleagues at the Center for Applied Special Technology (CAST) began exploring how to use new technologies to expand educational opportunities for learners of all abilities. Our work taught us that when education fails, barriers to learning are likely found in the curriculum—not in individual learners, who fall along a long continuum of diverse abilities, interests, and skills. As a result, the burden to adapt must, as a first step, be placed where it belongs: on the curriculum itself.

UNIVERSAL DESIGN FOR LEARNING

Grounded in research of learner differences, the capacities of new media, and the most effective teaching practices and assessments, UDL provides a framework for creating more robust learning opportunities for everyone. Emerging educational technologies, which are remarkably flexible, can support such new approaches to learning and teaching in ways that are impossible in a curriculum based entirely on print and lecture (Meyer & Rose, 2005).

As science reveals new findings about how learning happens in the brain, we can apply those insights to education. Brain imaging technologies allow us to "see" the brain as it learns by performing enormously complicated computations on subtle changes in brain activity that are then displayed on a computer screen. They confirm the vast variety of learners' abilities—and undermine efforts to shoehorn learners into standardized, one-size-fits-all approaches. Such technologies enable us to actually see the activity in three elaborate sets of nerve networks that play a primary role in learning.

Building on the work of Russian psychologist Lev Vygotsky (1978), we refer to these three nerve networks as the recognition, strategic, and affective networks to reflect their individual specializations. Briefly,

- Recognition networks are specialized to receive and analyze information (the "what" of learning);
- Strategic networks are specialized to plan and execute actions (the "how" of learning);
- Affective networks are specialized to evaluate and set priorities (the "why" of learning).

Collectively, these networks coordinate how we work and learn. Likewise, the corresponding principles of UDL aim to minimize barriers and maximize learning by flexibly accommodating individual differences in recognition, strategy, or affect, respectively:

- To support students who are diverse in learning to recognize their world, provide multiple, flexible methods of presentation;
- To support students who are diverse in learning strategies for action, provide multiple, flexible methods of expression and apprenticeship;

TABLE 1   UDL Principles

Brain Networks	UDL Response To anticipate differences in these networks
Recognition networks make it possible to receive and analyze information—i.e., to recognize patterns, concepts, and relationships. This is the "what" of learning.	Provide multiple, flexible methods of *presentation*. Give learners various ways to acquire information and knowledge.
Strategic networks make it possible to generate patterns and develop strategies for action and problem-solving. This is the "how" of learning.	Provide multiple, flexible methods of *expression* and apprenticeship. Offer students alternatives for demonstrating what they know.
Affective networks fuel motivation and guide the ability to establish priorities, focus attention, and choose action. This is the "why" of learning.	Provide multiple, flexible options for *engagement* in order to help learners get interested, be challenged, and stay motivated.

Source: Rose and Meyer (2000, 2002)

- To support students who are diverse in what motivates them to engage and sustain effort, provide multiple, flexible options for engagement (Rose & Meyer, 2000, 2002).

These UDL principles guide curriculum developers and teachers in applying the flexibility of digital media to create curriculum with built-in adjustability so that each learner finds the content and level of challenge and support that's right for him or her.

WHY THIS BOOK?

Of course, the real challenge is to put these principles into practice at the classroom level. The concerns of classroom teachers and the wisdom they share have shaped our definition of the principles and guided our UDL research at CAST. CAST works with school practitioners through our National Consortium on Universal Design for Learning, a virtual community of educators who share ideas and information; through our professional development with states, districts, and postsecondary institutions throughout the United States; through UDL institutes; and in our classroom research projects, where teachers help us develop more inclusive and effective learning environments.

Skilled and dedicated teachers are essential to making a universally designed curriculum successful: They are the ultimate source of customized teaching and support. Good teachers make adjustments all the time to accommodate diverse learner needs. The UDL framework helps them do so more effectively. Several articles collected here emphasize the central place education practitioners have in any meaningful reform.

The importance of digital learning environments is also highlighted in this book, though a clarification of this point is in order. UDL is often mistaken for some kind of technology program, just as our organization, CAST, is misunderstood as a technology-development house. On the contrary, ours is a learning organization focused on finding ways to improve classroom learning and teaching. Universally designed, multimedia learning environments extend a teacher's ability to reach individual learners, something printed textbooks alone cannot do. New technologies are not themselves instructional. However, when combined with effective instructional methods in the UDL model, they offer extraordinary ways to customize learning and teaching. Articles on new learning environments and alternatives to the traditional textbook demonstrate such possibilities.

Finally, literacy is a cornerstone of CAST's work and therefore is a key theme of this reader. The reason for this is simple: Students need robust reading comprehension skills and strategies, both of print and digital texts, in order to succeed across a number of subject areas. In articles about the development of the Thinking Reader literacy environment, teaching Internet literacy strategies, and improving adolescent literacy we highlight best practices and classroom-based research in Universal Design for Learning. In recent years, CAST has expanded its research into subjects such as science, mathematics, and history, as well as postsecondary learning. The innovations in classroom literacy discussed in this volume have produced fertile soil in which to plant these other projects.

REFERENCES

Meyer, A., & Rose, D. H. (2005). The future is in the margins: The role of technology and disability in educational reform. In D. H. Rose, A. Meyer, & C. Hitchcock (Eds.), *The universally designed classroom: Accessible curriculum and digital technologies*. Cambridge, MA: Harvard Education Press.

Rose, D., & Meyer, A. (2000). Universal design for individual differences. *Educational Leadership, 58*(3), 39–43.

Rose, D. H., & Meyer, A. (2002). *Teaching every student in the digital age: Universal design for learning*. Alexandria, VA: ASCD. (Also available in digital format at http://www.cast.org.)

Vygotsky, L. S. (1978). *Mind and society: The development of higher mental processes*. Cambridge, MA: Harvard University Press.

CHAPTER ONE

Applying Universal Design for Learning in the Classroom

PEGGY COYNE, PATRICIA GANLEY, TRACEY HALL, GRACE MEO, ELIZABETH MURRAY, AND DAVID GORDON

INTRODUCTION

What does Universal Design for Learning (UDL) look like in the classroom? We are often confronted with that question in our professional development, research, and policy work. We ask ourselves the same question because we know that practitioners don't need another "flavor-of-the-month" program or framework that looks good in theory but doesn't work on Monday morning. We also know that UDL looks different in every classroom. Since it discusses neuroscience and theories of learning, the research literature on UDL at times seems highly theoretical. UDL is also often misunderstood as a technology-only approach. Yet our work in professional development, research, and policy all points toward a distinct goal: supporting and improving instruction for all learners in today's classroom.

In this chapter, we share some observations gleaned from classrooms in which teachers have started to implement UDL. After a brief description of the UDL principles, we show how the application of these principles in inclusive classroom settings helps teachers recognize barriers to learning, strategically address such barriers, and monitor student progress. Finally, we conclude with some lessons about the role of technology in the UDL classroom.

THE UDL APPROACH

The principles of UDL are derived from the research and development of new learning environments by CAST and others during the past two decades. Inspired by universal design in architecture and the extensiveness of individual differences, UDL is an approach to designing instructional methods and materials that are flexible enough from the outset to accommodate learner differences (Meyer & Rose, 1998, 2005; Rose & Meyer, 2000, 2002).

UDL synthesizes—or at the very least complements—a number of educational approaches with which teachers may already be familiar. It draws on and extends effective teaching practices to customize instruction. For example, UDL emphasizes teachers as coaches or guides (O'Donnell, 1998), learning as process (Graves, Cooke, & Laberge, 1983), cooperative learning (Johnson & Johnson, 1986; Wood, Algozzine, & Avett, 1993), and reciprocal teaching for literacy (Palincsar & Brown, 1986). UDL is also a way to differentiate instruction (Tomlinson, 1999). In these approaches, teachers support learning rather than impart knowledge; students construct knowledge rather than passively receive it.

UDL represents a shift in how we look at learner differences. It emphasizes the need for curriculum that can adapt to student needs rather than require adaptation from the learners. It helps us identify and remove barriers in the curriculum. Equally important, it helps us identify and leverage individual learners' strengths. UDL provides a framework for setting clear learning goals for each learner, selecting and implementing flexible materials, providing instruction that challenges and supports each learner, and assessing each learner's progress more accurately (Meyer & Rose, 2005).

The UDL framework builds on the work of Lev Vygotsky (1978) and on recent advances in the neurosciences in learning the way the brain processes information. Vygotsky argued that learning is made up of three essential elements: recognition of the information to be learned, application of strategies to process that information, and engagement with the learning task. Brain imaging studies conducted while individuals are performing learning tasks (reading, writing, etc.) reveal three distinct neural networks at work in the learning brain: recognition networks, strategic networks, and affective networks (Rose & Meyer, 2002). Accordingly, UDL offers three guiding principles for developing curricula that eliminate barriers to learning, build on student strengths, and allow different ways to succeed:

1. To support diverse recognition networks, provide multiple means of *representation*
2. To support diverse strategic networks, provide multiple means of *action and expression*
3. To support diverse affective networks, provide multiple means of *engagement*

Recognition networks allow us to gather facts and information—the "what" of learning. They guide the collection and identification of the stimuli that we perceive. For example, the causes of the Civil War, how photosynthesis works, and the difference between adverbs and adjectives are all patterns to be recognized. Because of differences in individual recognition networks, there can be great variation in how each learner processes information. Offering *multiple means of representation*, including a variety of formats, will provide diverse learners with the opportunity to acquire the information and knowledge necessary to succeed in class.

Strategic networks aid us in planning and performing tasks, essentially in choosing a strategy for our actions—the "how" of learning. Solving an arithmetic problem, composing a book report, and taking notes in class are all strategic tasks. Differences in strategic networks mean that the ways students prefer to express their knowledge will vary greatly. Offering students *multiple means of action and expression* enables them to demonstrate most effectively what they have learned.

Affective networks determine our engagement, motivation, interest, and emotional connection—the "why" of learning. Motivation, meaning-making, and emotional involvement originate in the affective networks. Providing *multiple means of engagement* is necessary to motivate learners with widely varying affective networks, and thus varying interests. Of course, students often do not get to choose what to learn—that's determined by standards, by the curriculum, or by the teacher—but the more choice they have for ways of engaging with that mandatory material, the more likely it is that some element of the curriculum will challenge students appropriately and motivate them to learn (Rose & Meyer, 2002).

In practical terms, these principles are applied to all facets of instruction, including learning goals, methods, assessment, and materials. Based on our work with teachers, we and our colleagues at CAST have developed a set of teaching methods to guide educators in applying them. While these methods are by no means comprehensive—they are not the *only* means of universally designing instruction—they do offer a helpful checklist from which to work (Table 1).

PLANNING FOR ALL LEARNERS

An initial step in applying UDL is to identify and remove barriers in the curriculum. One primary means of accomplishing this is to set clear goals for student learning from the outset. What is the instructional goal of this lesson? In many cases, a starting point will be the predefined goals or standards required by the district or state. But that is only a beginning. Standards may spell out what students need to learn, but on closer examination one can often see that measuring "what" is learned can be impeded by unclear goals that define "how" that goal is to be achieved, thereby excluding certain numbers of learners. Thus it is essential when defining the goal to separate the means for reaching it from the goal itself.

For example, a learning goal for high schoolers may be to have them understand the causes of the Civil War. If the stated goal is that "By the end of this unit, every student will read chapter two in the textbook and will write an essay on the origins of the Civil War," students who struggle to read and write will be at a disadvantage from the outset in demonstrating their knowledge. Those whose disabilities make decoding text difficult, or make it hard to organize an essay, may not even be able to participate.

TABLE 1   UDL Teaching Methods

To Support Diverse Recognition Networks

- Provide multiple examples.
- Highlight critical features.
- Provide multiple media and formats.
- Support background context.

To Support Diverse Strategic Networks

- Provide flexible models of skilled performance.
- Provide opportunities to practice with supports.
- Provide ongoing, relevant feedback.
- Offer flexible opportunities for demonstrating skill.

To Support Diverse Affective Networks

- Offer choices of learning context.
- Offer choices of content and tools.
- Offer adjustable levels of challenge.
- Offer multiple ways to be successful.

Source: Rose and Meyer (2002)

The UDL framework provides teachers with an opportunity to re-think the unit goal, analyze its true intent, and adjust the way the goal is articulated to refocus attention on the content rather than on the methods used to express that knowledge. Is reading a printed text the only way to acquire the information? Is it important that students demonstrate what they know in a particular medium—writing an essay—or are there other ways to communicate their understanding?

Once we clarify the real purpose of the lesson and its activities, we can plan broadly enough to include all students, knowing that supports and scaffolds will be needed to help some students participate, and additional methods will be needed to enable other students to progress to new levels. Establishing a clear goal helps teachers determine how to develop flexible learning environments that open the door for more students' participation and success. For example, a UDL goal for the Civil War unit may be restated to say that "By the end of the unit, all students will demonstrate an understanding of the origins of the Civil War."

We've found that teachers move from concept to practice most effectively by discussing UDL principles in the context of their own specific classroom and curriculum challenges. This works best as a back-and-forth process, as teachers jointly plan, analyze, and refine actual classroom lessons. In some ways, this echoes the "lesson study" model, the professional development favored by Japanese teachers and now used increasingly in North America (Lewis, 2002). With supportive coaching and time for reflective analysis, teachers learn to identify potential barriers for students at both individual and group levels, and to incorporate accommodations and adaptations in their instruction.

A school culture that values innovation in the service of reaching more learners is essential to UDL. This inevitably requires providing the time for planning and encouraging some risk-taking as teachers identify barriers and potential solutions. The process of lesson planning—especially the reflective kind—always seems to take longer than teachers anticipate. It requires some flexibility on the part of teachers in setting aside time to talk about what is happening in their classrooms, and it also requires the willingness to adjust curricular goals, methods, materials, and assessments.

INSTRUCTION THAT SUPPORTS DIVERSE LEARNERS

Teachers need flexible teaching methods to provide the multiple means of representation, expression, and engagement necessary. For example, to support recognition networks, they can provide multiple examples of concepts to be learned, highlight critical features, and help students build an understanding of background context.

For example, when Ms. Landers,* a teacher at an inner-city K–8 school, chose to include Chinua Achebe's *Things Fall Apart* in her seventh-grade curriculum, she realized that the novel posed barriers for her

---

*All teachers' names have been changed to protect their confidentiality as research participants.

students. One significant barrier was background knowledge. In order to help students understand the novel's complex themes and imagery, Ms. Landers needed to build their knowledge about precolonial Nigeria and the Igbo people. She collaborated with Mr. Appiah, the social studies teacher, who taught a unit on precolonial Nigeria and the Igbo culture before students read the novel.

The approach was successful. Students were better able to make more connections and understand why certain events in the book happened. For example, a scene in the novel describes the evil forest and the clay jars containing the bodies of twin babies. The students could now connect this description to the Igbo belief that multiple births are unnatural, and understand that different cultures have different beliefs.

In a suburban middle school class, teachers faced a similar challenge. The students were scheduled to read *Number the Stars,* a Holocaust novel by Lois Lowry. The special education teacher constructed and presented a PowerPoint presentation with timelines and charts describing the Holocaust; the English language arts teacher drafted a short play based on the first chapter for students to perform. Both the resource and the activity gave students a better understanding of the novel's complex characters and settings before they began to read.

UDL teaching is interactive and learner-centered, with an emphasis on learning concepts—rather than a traditional teacher-directed style emphasizing facts and figures. Of course, this is not to suggest that the teacher is any less essential in the UDL classroom; she or he may be *more* essential, since the job requires much more than simply transmitting information. UDL was developed as a way to support and build teacher expertise. In turn, teachers guide students in scaffolding their own skills, knowledge, and expertise to become lifelong learners.

MATERIALS THAT SUPPORT ALL LEARNERS

Providing students with choices and flexibility in their materials and assignments is essential to UDL implementation. This supports the development of diverse recognition networks by providing students with multiple views of the material in question—and therefore making it more likely that learners will identify important facts, features, and trends—it supports the development of diverse strategic networks by giving learners multiple ways of approaching a challenging task, and it supports the development of diverse affective networks by making it more likely that students will sense some ownership of their learning since they can approach tasks in ways that work best for them.

For example, in one middle school language arts classroom using UDL, students were assigned the task of "becoming the expert" on ancient Mesopotamia and asked to share their knowledge with the class. They were given a variety of choices of ways to accomplish this. They took this responsibility very seriously, and committed to research and present information to the best of their ability. Suddenly, ancient Mesopotamia, a potentially dull and unconnected subject for sixth graders, elicited immense enthusiasm. Students worked in groups and individually. They wrote newspaper articles; wrote, directed, and filmed television news programs; performed puppet shows and plays; created posters; or wrote research papers. They then presented their work to the class. Having choices of expression gave students more opportunity and greater incentive to develop expert products, thereby becoming more active as learners.

Expanding the audience and the purpose for student output is another method teachers used to meet the needs of more students. In one UDL class, students used a blog to discuss difficult issues brought up in literature they were reading. They shared their opinions. They also uploaded their work so that their peers could comment on it. In another class, students created an anthology of their poetry, artwork, and artist/poet notes in response to novels they read in a unit on the Holocaust. They proudly donated a copy to the school library. In a middle-school science class, a teacher created a new assignment for her human anatomy unit: building a working joint. The teacher posted this assignment on the school website and invited parents to work with their students in fulfilling it. The resulting models—made from PVC pipes, rubber bands, bungee cords, door hinges, and other household items—were put on display in the school for the community to view. Building the joint and seeing multiple examples of the completed project helped students better understand this complex anatomical concept. As an added bonus, parents got involved in the assignment, too, and came to school to view the other models.

Technology-based approaches often provide effective ways to customize learning for students with diverse needs, abilities, and styles. At Ms. Landers's urban K–8 school, that language arts teacher addressed her seventh graders' dramatic differences in reading ability by using digital novels loaded with rich supports in combination with traditional printed books. These universally designed Thinking Reader® editions (Tom Snyder Productions/Scholastic) include a variety of supports and scaffolds. In addition to giving students background knowledge and vocabulary support at certain points, they prompted them to think strategically about their reading and respond to questions about the text. Animated characters act as skilled mentors, offering model responses and giving students feedback about their own responses. These interactions are captured in online worklogs so that teachers and students together can assess how students are performing. As a result, more students in Ms. Landers's class had an opportunity to read the full text of *Bud, Not Buddy* and other award-winning books.

Meanwhile, at the suburban middle school, Ms. Casey developed her own digitally supported text to use with her eighth-grade social studies class. Working with CAST researchers, she embedded electronic vocabulary, background knowledge, and reading comprehension supports into a digital version of the book, *Saladin, Noble Prince of Islam*. Students used the book to study the Crusades. Ms. Casey opted to create this digital book because several of her students struggle greatly with reading, while others need the engagement that using technology can provide.

INCREASING STUDENT ENGAGEMENT

UDL gives teachers a framework for developing engaging learning environments. By providing students with multiple pathways for reaching a common goal, teachers are more likely to engage and motivate their students. Data from student interviews and surveys support our team's observations of high levels of student engagement as all students reach for a common goal. Students report substantially more enthusiasm for and engagement in projects that provide choices of topic, presentation, and expression. Teachers also report a correlation between the level of student engagement and the quality of work.

In schools where we have worked, teachers who began to offer more choices of topics and means of assessment noticed that a broader range of students were able to participate. Also, as students became more engaged in the curriculum, they put more time and effort into their work. This, in turn, raised teachers' expectations for that work. By the end of the year, teachers were expecting students to commit more time and energy to the assignments. In language arts, the teacher assigned students to demonstrate their understanding of the various genres that had been studied during the year by developing presentations on a topic of their choice. The teacher incorporated provided models, grading rubrics, and other student supports to scaffold their work. Students chose topics ranging from John Deere's life to soccer in America. The teacher was awed by the quality of the presentations her students produced.

In one sense, this should seem obvious: most of us, including students, like to have some choice and control in our lives. Yet so often schools' one-size-fits-all approach eliminates the very thing that might engage and motivate many learners: choice.

UDL AND TECHNOLOGY

UDL is an approach to creating more flexible teaching and learning experiences. Of course, the means that schools have to accomplish this can vary widely. As the examples in this article demonstrate, educational technology can help teachers create more flexible learning environments—but they are not the only way to do so. A printed book represents a certain kind of technology, yet we know that having access to books is not the same as learning from books. Similarly, providing students with access to computers, the Web, blogs, iPods, and other technologies is not the same as providing access to learning. Educators who do not have access to the latest multimedia and computer-based technologies can still apply UDL in powerful ways.

UDL gives educators a context for using technology effectively. In our work with teachers, we have worked with them to develop expertise in using computer-based technology appropriately with students—but to do so with the ultimate goal of making the learning environment more flexible and effective. At times this work has led to the development of new tools that support and individualize instruction and learning. It has also led to creative and innovative uses of readily available classroom technologies.

Educators need to beware that technology does not become a distraction to achieving the goal. For example, issues will arise when implementing any new software in the classroom. After the teachers we worked with became more comfortable with the technology, they began to realize that UDL is more than just about the technology—that they were more successful when they combined technology with UDL practices like providing background information, models, and choices of topics for assessment. Looking back, we now see the necessity of creating a foundation of UDL teaching practices and methods before introducing a new technology.

Once they have grasped UDL principles and incorporated them into their teaching, many teachers find that technology tools provide them with many more options for supporting all learners. For example, three teachers we worked with (grades 4–5) chose to digitize two novels and load them with supports for students with poor decoding skills. Learning prompts for each novel were embedded directly into the text. Embedded supports included a character web using an Inspiration® template, and prompts that asked students to respond to comprehension strategies such as summarizing, predicting, questioning, visualizing, and identifying how characters were feeling at important points in the stories.

Very early on, teachers recognized that digital text with embedded supports could assist specific students in their classes. The teachers used the technology not as the choice and solution for all, but rather as the choice and solution for some. Teachers were very adept at identifying which students benefited from the technology, and they never assumed that all students would use the technology for all assignments. They understood that computers were one choice among many approaches to curriculum and instruction. By the end of that year, the teachers had become more effective at developing strategies for instruction in case the technology didn't work. This practice evolved into planning UDL lessons with more flexibility and options. Teachers began to view technology as one of many tools for instruction.

In her seventh-grade class, Ms. Landers offered students more choices of ways to demonstrate their understanding and knowledge. One group of students used the software program Hollywood High to create an animated movie depicting a scene from Gary Soto's novel, *Taking Sides*. Ms. Landers also made the software program Write: OutLoud® available to students who needed the immediate speech feedback while writing. She encouraged her students to try using different tools and strategies to see which would help them be more successful.

Initially, the novelty of UDL planning and technology required high levels of concentration and focus for teachers in classrooms where CAST worked. As they became more familiar with both the technology tools and UDL principles, the teachers themselves were more effective and could focus more on the instructional episode and content instead of the technology itself.

CONCLUSION

The UDL framework supports all learners by providing equitable and effective education. UDL instructional goals, methods, materials, and assessments simultaneously lower barriers to learning and build on learner strengths. As this article demonstrates, there are numerous practical steps instructors can take in everyday settings, with and without technology, to improve the learning experience of all of their students and to support their educational progress.

REFERENCES

Graves, M. F., Cooke, C. L., & Laberge, M. J. (1983). Effects of previewing difficult short stories on low ability junior high school students' comprehension, recall, and attitudes. *Reading Research Quarterly, 18,* 262–276.

Johnson, D. W., & Johnson, R. T. (1986). Mainstreaming and cooperative learning strategies. *Exceptional Children, 52,* 552–561.

Lewis, C. (2002). *Lesson study: A handbook for teacher-led improvement of instruction.* Philadelphia: Research for Better Schools.

Meyer, A., & Rose, D. H. (1998). *Learning to read in the computer age* (Vol. 3). Cambridge, MA: Brookline Books.

Meyer, A., & Rose, D. H. (2005). The future is in the margins: The role of technology and disability in educational reform. In D. H. Rose, A. Meyer, & C. Hitchcock (Eds.), *The universally designed classroom: Accessible curriculum and digital technologies* (pp. 13–36). Cambridge, MA: Harvard Education Press.

O'Donnell, J. J. (1998). *Avatars of the word: From papyrus to cyberspace.* Cambridge, MA: Harvard University Press.

Palincsar, A. S., & Brown, A. L. (1986). Interactive teaching to promote independent learning from text. *The Reading Teacher, 39,* 771–777.

Rose, D., & Meyer, A. (2000). Universal design for individual differences. *Educational Leadership, 58*(3), 39–43.

Rose, D. H., & Meyer, A. (2002). *Teaching every student in the digital age: Universal design for learning.* Alexandria, VA: ASCD.

Tomlinson, C. (1999). *The differentiated classroom: Responding to the needs of all learners.* Alexandria, VA: ASCD.

Vygotsky, L. S. (1978). *Mind and society: The development of higher mental processes.* Cambridge, MA: Harvard University Press.

Wood, K. D., Algozzine, B., & Avett, S. (1993). Promoting cooperative learning experiences for students with reading, writing, and learning disabilities. *Reading and Writing Quarterly, 9,* 369–376.

CHAPTER TWO

A UDL Case Story and Model Lesson: Reading Challenges in Geography and Social Studies

THE STAFF AT CAST

UDL CASE STORY

Dilemma

Ms. Jones, a fourth-grade teacher, is concerned that her students' diverse reading abilities prevent them from understanding social studies material and achieving the standards set for their grade level, particularly since she only has forty-five minutes per day for social studies instruction.

Ms. Jones has twenty-nine students: fourteen girls and fifteen boys. Her students represent a heterogeneous mix of backgrounds and abilities. She has six students who have identified disabilities and an Individualized Education Plan (IEP). Of these six students, four have a specific learning disability, and two have speech and language disabilities. Four other students are English-language learners. In addition, there is a great diversity of reading ability across the classroom population, particularly in the areas of decoding, comprehension, and language. Although Ms. Jones can provide instruction for groups and individuals that accommodates individual needs during the 1½-hour language arts time, the 45-minute time allocation for social studies does not allow time to differentiate instruction.

School and Classroom Setting

Ms. Jones teaches in a school that has made a commitment to focus on improving students' reading skills by increasing the amount of instructional time allocated for reading. The faculty is philosophically committed to inclusion, and her students represent a heterogeneous mix of backgrounds. This includes students with specific learning disabilities, speech and language disabilities, English-language learners, and students who have widely diverse reading abilities.

Her school contains instructional materials, computers, and Internet access similar to the other fourteen elementary schools in her district. She teaches in a suburban district located northwest of Chicago. The district has a total school population of 11,500 students, of which approximately 1,500 have identified disabilities. The district goal is to upgrade facilities built between 1969 and 1985 to provide appropriate technology for instructional use and faculty/staff support.

Decisions about placement in the least restrictive environment for students with disabilities are made on an individual basis by IEP teams, and in consultation with each student's parents. In addition, the faculty has adopted a commitment to focus on improving reading skills by increasing the allocation of instructional time for reading and language arts and, therefore, reducing time allocations in other subject areas. The curriculum and student goals are aligned with state standards, and students are formally tested in grades 5, 8, and 10.

The Media Center is equipped with six desktop computers with Internet access, and Ms. Jones's classroom houses two computers with broadband Internet connections and software for word processing, spreadsheet manipulation, and graphics processing.

Ms. Jones is a veteran teacher in the district. She has taught in this school for eleven of her fourteen years of teaching at the upper elementary level. She holds a master's degree in elementary education, and specializes in reading and language arts. She is viewed as a committed teacher who wants her students to be successful. She embraces students with individual differences, and strives to adapt her teaching to each new group of students.

When the school made a commitment to the inclusion of students with disabilities in the general education classrooms, she fully support-

TABLE 1   Overview of Ms. Jones's School

Administration	Principal and Vice Principal
Grades housed in building	K–5
Student population	675
Classes and teachers per grade	2–3
Special education teachers	2 full-time
	1 part-time (speech and language)
Support staff (paraprofessionals)	6
Socioeconomic status	57% free and reduced-price lunch
Title I funding	Schoolwide
Percent of student population with identified disabilities	Approximately 11%

ed that initiative. She attended several summer workshops on inclusion, and attends the IEP meetings for each of the six students in her class who has identified disabilities. Ms. Jones reaches out to each of her students in an effort to meet his or her individual needs.

The twenty-nine students in Ms. Jones's class have very diverse reading abilities; they are organized into four homogeneous reading groups for the daily reading instruction. Instructional time for reading is 1½ hours per day. Ms. Jones has one paraprofessional in the classroom.

The resources in Ms. Jones's fourth-grade class are typical of a district elementary school. She has two computers available for teacher and student use, with broadband Internet connections and standard software for word processing, spreadsheet manipulation, and graphics processing. There is a complete encyclopedia available, both in print and electronically on CD-ROM.

Students use the print version of the district-adopted social studies textbook. Each student has a textbook, and a paraprofessional is available for thirty minutes per day during the reading instruction time.

Curriculum: Goals

Ms. Jones has thought carefully about the goals, or intended outcomes, for her social studies lesson. She knows that the standards developed by national, state, and local curriculum groups are what her students must know and be able to do, and she is aware that she is responsible for creating goals and objectives that determine the design and direction of every element in the curriculum—how media and materials will be selected, how instruction will be implemented, and how student progress will be evaluated.

For this lesson, her goal is to engage her students in doing research on a region's physical and topographical characteristics in order to draw a map. She plans to expand her traditional instructional methods to include a Universal Design for Learning (UDL) approach. She is particularly interested in structuring her lesson to help students become more proficient in doing research and to improve their ability to read social studies text material.

Ms. Jones knows that standards are a statement of what is valued in education, and that they determine what teachers teach and assess. Standards, which are usually developed by national, state, and local curriculum groups, are designed to articulate the knowledge, skills, and understandings all students should achieve. Ms. Jones knows that she must create goals and objectives to articulate and plan steps toward meeting prescribed standards, and that she must clearly communicate these learning goals to her students.

For Ms. Jones, the relevant standards are those developed by the National Council of Social Studies (NCSS), and are further articulated in the Illinois state standards:

NCSS Standard III (People, Places, and Environments): *Social studies programs should include experiences that provide for the study of people, places, and environments.* (See model lesson for complete details.)

Illinois standards for fourth grade:

The geographically informed person knows and understands:

Standard 2: How to use mental maps to organize information about people, places, and environments in a spatial context.
  Knowledge Statement 3—The location of major physical and human features in the United States and on Earth.

Standard 5: That people create regions to interpret Earth's complexity.
Knowledge Statement 2—The similarities and differences among regions.

Standard 12: The processes, patterns, and functions of human settlement.
Knowledge Statement 2—The factors that affect where people settle.

Ms. Jones designs instructional goals for the unit that are linked to the standards and that are specific to content and learning activities. From these standards, she can shape the lesson goals and individualize the means for attaining them.

Traditional Approach
1. Student groups create a map containing political, topographical, and natural resources in the selected state of study.
2. Students will orally present and describe the state and map results to the class.

UDL Approach
1. Students map the political, topographical, and natural resources of a selected state.
2. Students present results to demonstrate understandings of the state and its resources.

Ms. Jones writes instructional objectives for individual lessons to specify student expectations and clarify steps toward meeting the standards' goals.

Traditional Approach
1. Read the social studies text and (a minimum of) two additional resources to gather information about state resources, geography, and political structures.
2. Write a compare-and-contrast table of state resources.
3. Make a representative map using available materials.
4. Present information to the class.
5. Raise hands to answer teacher and presenter questions on the presentation.

UDL Approach
1. The students will (a) collect information, (b) make comparisons, and (c) create maps to represent state resources, topography, and political information.
2. Present information to the class. Analyze information and respond to questions.

Curriculum: Methods

Methods are the actions the teacher takes to facilitate student learning. Ms. Jones expands her traditional instructional approaches to teaching this lesson to include UDL approaches. She has decided that the methodology for this lesson should be divided into three sections: Introduce, Guide, and Close.

She first considers what a traditional lesson presentation should be, and then determines ways in which the lesson could be universally designed. Her goal is to make the lesson more accessible and flexible for the diversity of students in her classroom.

Introduce the Lesson

Ms. Jones will begin by introducing the topic and making connections to previous instruction.

Traditional Approach
1. The teacher provides a brief lecture on the home state. She reminds students of previous studies of land and resources, and the impact of natural resources on population growth, political, and land-use issues.
2. The teacher divides the students into working groups to complete their research, map-making, note-taking, and presentation.

UDL Approach
1. Avoid limiting presentation style. There may be students who do not respond, comprehend, or attend well to a lecture style. Consider the use of media with the presentation (e.g., concept maps or graphics) to enhance and illustrate concepts and topics that are introduced and reviewed.
2. When opening the lesson, consider frequent questions and statements of clarification; solicit student participation.

3. Consider assigning students to working groups by mixed abilities (heterogeneous grouping) to make use of complementary skills.
4. Provide demonstrations of performance expectations.

Guide the Lesson-Learning

In the main body of the lesson, Ms. Jones engages the students in the core content and concepts, and she involves them in practice and/or producing work products.

Traditional Approach: Research

1. Students read the textbook chapter on the selected home state to find out about the state resources, boundaries, topography, and population centers. Students are required to use at least one outside resource.
2. Student groups must also take written notes to support their research work.

UDL Approach: Research

1. Provide multiple means to access resource materials.
2. Scaffold reading with supports for decoding and vocabulary.
3. Support reading strategies with cooperative working groups (e.g., paired reading, discussion sessions).
4. Consider alternative means for note-taking (e.g., audio-recorded summary, electronic note-taking).
5. Scaffold note-taking by allowing students to use a graphic organizer with information prompts built in (e.g., name of state, land mass, geographic location).

Close the Lesson

Ms. Jones closes the lesson with summative activities or tasks that review where students began, what they learned, and how this lesson relates to future lessons.

Traditional Approach

1. Using the map, groups give oral presentations, including resource information, to the class.
2. Each student takes notes during the presentations.
3. Students draw and write a compare/contrast chart of the physical, political, and geographical characteristics of the states presented by all groups.

UDL Approach

1. Provide students with options for presenting information (e.g., presentation may be written, oral, video, or visual).
2. Provide audience with scaffolds and alternative means of collecting information as students make presentations (e.g., recording, notes, response questions).
3. Consider alternatives for writing a compare/contrast chart (e.g., oral, pictorial, digital).

Curriculum: Media and Materials

Media and materials are the backbone of a curriculum; they embody its purpose. The facts, concepts, information, principles, and relationships that are to be learned must be represented in media that communicate effectively to students, and stored and distributed in media that are accessible to all learners.

Media are the means of symbolic or physical representation through which knowledge is communicated. The most common media in instructional settings include text, image, speech, video, sculpture, theater, etc. The UDL context differentiates between traditional or "fixed" media and digital media because digital media are flexible and can be adjusted.

Materials are the physical objects or devices that are used to store and distribute knowledge as it is conveyed in various media. Publications such as textbooks, trade books, videos, CD-ROMs, workbooks, floppy disks, and audiotapes are common examples of materials.

Ms. Jones uses traditional media and materials, as well as media and materials that support UDL implementation.

Traditional Approach

- Social studies textbook
- Encyclopedia
- Map materials
- Tag board
- Colored pencils
- Rulers
- Glue
- Clay

- Trays
- CD software on U.S. geography

UDL Approach
- Printed text may constitute a barrier for students with physical or reading disabilities. If texts are digitally available, teachers and students have options for text-to-speech, braille, and a variety of display formats.
- Provide various means and materials that students can use to create a map. Examples include: (a) draw a map; (b) create a map with clay, etc.; (c) create a map electronically with computer tools (GIS); (d) have students verbalize for others the details of what to place on a map and where.
- Some learners may have organizational deficits, making it challenging for them to understand and make use of library structure and thus the library resource. Provide scaffolds and instruction to find resource materials in multiple formats—text, digital, audio, etc.
  - Preselect possible materials for students to review/research;
  - Direct students to area of media center with appropriate resource materials;
  - Consider textbook barriers noted in "materials/classroom."
- Some learners may have difficulty using computers with a CD, hindering access to the resource material.
  - Provide supports and instruction to use of CD resource;
  - Evaluate access issues for vision, decoding, etc., for the various students in the class.

Curriculum: Assessment

Assessment is a method for determining a learner's knowledge and abilities and is used to make educational decisions. The teacher, testing agencies, or the government may design assessments. Universally designed assessments are designed to adjust to many individual differences and to focus the questions on exactly what teachers are trying to find out. Flexibility in presentation, expression, supports, and engagement reduces common errors introduced by single-mode fixed assessments. Furthermore, that same flexibility allows teachers to align assessment more closely with teaching goals and methods, and thus to assess students more accurately.

Ms. Jones understands that assessing student progress is a more comprehensive practice than simply preparing and giving a test. She knows that it is necessary to observe her students and provide feedback as they write, and to provide flexible structures, such as rubric scoring, to assess her students' progress.

Observe and Record

Assessment in a UDL lesson is the process of gathering information about a learner from his or her performance in a variety of tasks, subjects, and learning contexts to determine abilities and knowledge for the purpose of making educational decisions (adapted from Salvia & Ysseldyke, 2000). The teacher knows that one effective method of evaluating students' knowledge is to engage students in activities and assignments.

Traditional Approach
- Assign a grade to each component of the students' work:
  - The group-created map
  - The class presentation
  - Students' notes regarding presentations
  - Students' compare/contrast chart

UDL Approach
- Monitor cooperation in working groups and student roles. Provide instruction, scaffolds, and feedback.
- Observe and record learner use of notes and resources when completing the map.
- Observe and record student note-taking, using constructed or open-ended formats. Indicate type and accuracy of notes. Determine need for further instruction.
- Check map contents, organization, and presentation with prepared scoring rubric.

Evaluate Performance

Ms. Jones frequently uses tests and student products to evaluate students' understanding of new content.

Traditional Approach
- Administer the end-of-chapter test prepared by the textbook publisher and found in the Teacher's Guide. The test consists of multiple-choice questions and short-essay answers.

UDL Approach
- Evaluate the constructs measured in the published test. Determine if the lesson evaluation procedures match the lesson standards and goals.
- If this measure is determined adequate for the learning goals, evaluate the accessibility for all learners in the class.
- Consider alternative means of delivery, such as an oral test, providing untimed sessions, etc.

Conclusion

Ms. Jones has thought about her lesson both from the perspective of a traditional lesson presentation and from the perspective of Universal Design for Learning. She compares both approaches to help her decide how to work with her struggling readers in a 45-minute period.

Now she drafts her lesson plan.

UDL MODEL LESSON: GEOGRAPHY AND SOCIAL STUDIES

This UDL lesson was designed for teachers who are teaching a fourth-grade social studies unit that is mapped to state and national standards. The students are studying United States geography, learning the topographical, political, and natural resources information about their home (Illinois) and surrounding states. This lesson represents the second day of a six-day unit. The twenty-nine students in this fourth-grade classroom have very diverse reading skills. Based on schoolwide goals and schedules, the teacher has only forty-five minutes allocated for social studies instruction each day. All students must aim to meet the social studies state standards for grade 4, including proficiency in research, reading, note-taking, presentations, and map-making.

The unit objectives (measurable) state that students will:

1. Locate and indicate the physical and political features on a map of their selected state.
2. Make use of various informational sources (i.e., dictionary, encyclopedia, atlas, Internet) for research purposes.
3. Theorize about how physical features have influenced political features on a map (e.g., why are cities located where they are?).
4. Compare and contrast physical and political features of two or more bordering states.
5. Participate in a group presentation of prepared and researched report to the class.

The objectives for this particular lesson will address unit objectives 1, 2, and (partially) 3.

Lesson goals include:

1. Teacher uses Socratic method to review state of Illinois's physical features.
2. Teacher reviews regions with students.
3. Teacher models researching and illustrating Illinois's physical features.
4. Student groups research their state's physical features.
5. Students construct a visual representation of selected state.
6. Students informally share information about their state in comparison to Illinois.

The teacher has traditionally provided a lecture to introduce students to the topic, goals, and activities for the day. Students would then be divided into working groups and assigned tasks to research, to take notes, and to draw the state map depicting borders and physical characteristics of their assigned state.

In the UDL classroom, the teacher begins the lesson by using Illinois to demonstrate how to research and record information about a state. Then, the students work in cooperative groups, using their state fact-finding sheet to guide them through various information sources of their choosing during the research process. By the end of the lesson, students will have completed a draft of a physical map for their assigned state. Finally, the teacher and students will review the different types of information sources that can be used for research (i.e., encyclopedia, dictionary, atlas, Internet sources, etc.), and ask students if the state that they are researching has any similarities to Illinois.

Introduction

- (2 min.) Using a Socratic-style discussion, model and review Illinois's physical features with students.
  - Ask students about the physical features on maps (e.g., mountains, plateaus, lakes, rivers, plains, etc.).
  - Ask students to name specific physical features found in the United States (e.g., Mississippi River, Lake Erie, Great Salt Lake, Niagara Falls, Grand Canyon, Rocky Mountains, etc.).

- (3 min.) Display a map of the United States with simple physical and political features (projected map, wall map, etc).
  - Remind the students that physical features can determine regions on a map. For example, point out the Appalachian Mountains.
  - Using the map, ask students which states they think are part of the Appalachian region. (Kentucky, a state that borders Illinois, is part of this region.)
  - Point out the Great Lakes.
  - Ask the students which states are part of the Great Lakes Region. (Illinois is part of this region.)

Modeling/Guided Practice

- (10 min.) Use State Fact-Finding Tool: Physical Features to guide research for Illinois. Introduce the states checklist by posting it for all students.

Physical Features

  - Ask the students what type of resource they would use to find maps of states in the United States (e.g., atlas, textbook, Internet, CD, encyclopedia).
  - Remind students that together the class will practice researching and mapping physical features for Illinois. Then students will work in assigned groups to find the features of their selected state.
  - Project a map (with physical and political features) of Illinois on the wall.
  - Answer the first question on the State Fact-Finding Tool: Physical Features—What physical features are found in your state?

- Project an outline map of Illinois in juxtaposition to the physical feature map (in Draw Program).
- Use the Draw Tools to draw blue lines to represent the major bodies of water in Illinois (e.g., lakes and rivers).
- Label each major body of water. In the state of Illinois these include Illinois, Kaskaskia, Mississippi, Ohio, and Wabash rivers, and Lake Michigan.

Illinois's Climate
- Ask the students what resource they could use to find information about Illinois's climate (encyclopedia, textbook, Internet, Weather Channel).
- Display digital encyclopedia entry on Illinois's climate. Read this section aloud to the students.
- Ask students for adjectives they might use to describe Illinois's climate, using information from the encyclopedia. Record these adjectives on State Fact-Finding Tool: Physical Features.

Guided Practice
- (25 min.) Teacher asks students to move into previously assigned working groups and begin researching their selected state, based on the model provided by the teacher.
  - Teacher circulates throughout the room as student groups, using various chosen information resources, begin researching their state and recording information on their State Fact-Finding Tool: Physical Features and draft of state map.
  - All students have access to the checklist of steps to use to complete the assignment for this lesson (access includes wall chart, handout, digital copy, etc., of checklist).

Project Steps Checklist
- Select resources to research state.
- Use State Fact-Finding Tool and begin answering Question 1 about physical features.
- Select or develop outline of state.
- Indicate major bodies of water on map.
- Label major bodies of water.
- Research the climate of your state.

- Using the State Fact-Finding Tool and resources, answer Question 2 about state climate.

Materials/Tools
- Provide students with choices for representing their state's physical features:
    - Paper and pencil/pen
    - Draw program on computer
    - Construction paper and yarn (e.g., blue yarn represents rivers)
    - Clay
    - Other suggestions students make
- Provide students with choices of maps for research:
    - Website URLs
    - Encyclopedia
    - Traditional atlas
    - Maps in social studies textbook
- Provide students with choices of reading about Illinois's climate:
    - Partner with one of their team members

Conclusion

- (5 min.) Bring class back together to review the types of information resources and the types of information they supply. Informally ask the students to volunteer information about their state that is either similar to or different from that found in Illinois.

UDL Highlights

Recognition Supports

Provide multiple examples:
- Demonstrations by teacher of mapping features for home state
- Auditory and visual presentations of information
- Demonstrations to entire class and individual working groups
- Presentations, practice in small groups, regrouping and discussion/ sharing

Highlight critical features:
- Presentation and focus on single features of geography lesson (e.g., Day 2: Physical Features)
- Partially constructed maps from the Internet

Provide multiple media and formats:
- Multiple means to access resources (printed textbook, digital media, encyclopedia, textbook, Internet resources, etc.)
- Choices of media to complete research
- Choice of methods for assignment completion (computer, paper/pen, clay, etc.)
- Choice of presentation modes
- Choice of role in working/learning groups

Support background context:
- Demonstration of expectations with familiar content (home state)
- Cumulative review of previous lesson content building on new content
- URL with map-making guidelines

Strategic Supports

Teacher provides flexible models of skilled performance:
- Varying models of political and topographical maps
  - Globe
  - Wall map
  - Projection
  - Computer-designed
  - Clay or paper map
- Multiple methods of instruction in geography concepts
  - Large-group presentation/display
  - Oral presentations, demonstrations, descriptions
  - Mentoring/coaching student working groups
  - Visual-spatial displays from text and resources

- Teacher provides opportunities to practice with supports:
- Mapping skills in varying contexts
  - Large group
  - Student working groups
  - Individual

- Note-taking
  - Partially constructed note-taking worksheets (digital or paper)
  - Teacher prompting to note information during research
  - Paired and group supports during research

Teacher provides ongoing, relevant feedback:
  - Frequent checks with groups and individuals on tasks and activities
  - Monitoring and guiding student groups in decision-making, research, and product development

Teacher offers flexible opportunities for demonstrating skill:
  - Mapping
    - Choices of medium to construct map (computer, paper, clay, etc.)
    - Choice of state (state bordering Illinois)
  - Note-taking
    - Choice of medium to take notes (e.g., paper/pencil, keyboarding, scribing, audio taping)
    - Use of scaffolded note-taking worksheets (paper or digital available)
  - Choice of presentation style
    - Oral
    - Written
    - Visual/audio
    - Paper, diorama

Affective Supports

Teacher offers choices of content and tools:
  - Choices of particular bordering state to research
  - Options for how to obtain resource information
  - Choices of tool and medium to complete map
  - Choices of working-group roles
  - Options for presentation of materials to class

Teacher offers adjustable levels of challenge:
  - Scaffolded note-taking devices
  - Flexible presentation structure, depending on varied challenge levels
  - Supports and opportunities for collaboration in working groups
  - Partially constructed state map with state border

Teacher offers choices of learning context:
- Options for note-taking
- Choices of states to research
- Options for role and membership in working groups

Teacher offers engagement opportunities:
- Varied tools to engage and practice new content and mapping
- Demonstration to practice lesson structure that allows for engagement throughout the series of lessons

Reflections

The key to executing this lesson successfully is preparation. Fortunately, Ms. Jones was able to set up her school's media lab before she started teaching: the computer and LCD projector were ready to go, and Internet sites were accessed and minimized for the modeling portion.

She prepared stations for those students who opted for text-to-speech, teacher read-aloud, or silent-reading choices. Fortunately, her students were familiar with the computer's drawing program, so those who chose to use this option to construct their maps required little additional instruction.

Of course, lessons don't always go as planned. Ms. Jones took longer than the five minutes scheduled for the introduction. However, she was able to use a few minutes of the time she had allotted for guided practice (i.e., cooperative groups' research time).

Ms. Jones takes seriously the mandates specified by No Child Left Behind. She has found that teaching lessons using a UDL approach allows her to consider each student's individual learning needs and allows her to provide scaffolds and supports to ensure that the student can achieve the lesson goals. Her classroom is a hive of productive activity, a place where hard work, cooperation, confidence, and success are clearly evident.

REFERENCE

Salvia, J., & Ysseldyke, J. E. (2000). *Assessment* (8th ed.) Boston: Houghton Mifflin.

CHAPTER THREE

Frequent Questions about Universal Design for Learning

GRACE MEO

In recent years, Universal Design for Learning (UDL) has gained currency in educational practice and policy as a means of improving education for all learners, including those with disabilities. For example, the 2004 reauthorization of the Individuals with Disabilities Education Act (IDEA) "requires [that] state and districtwide tests adhere to 'universal design principles' to the extent feasible."

Meanwhile, states such as Kentucky, Louisiana, Ohio, Maryland, and New York are providing training and support to school personnel to apply UDL to curriculum development, technology planning, and classroom practice. In one pilot program, the state of Kentucky is supporting UDL implementation in 100 middle schools with professional training, digital textbooks and other accessible curricular materials, and technology assistance.

UDL blends insights from recent brain research and advances in multimedia to provide a blueprint for developing flexible instructional goals, methods, materials, and assessments that supports many kinds of learners in standards-based, inclusive classrooms. While many educators may be familiar with UDL, misconceptions persist.

Grace Meo, director of professional development programs and out-reach services at CAST, identifies and responds to some questions commonly raised by teachers and administrators about UDL.

Is UDL a software program or a curriculum? Is it something my school has to buy?

UDL is an approach to classroom planning and practice, not a shrink-wrapped package. It is a way of thinking about students, teaching, and curriculum—a way of recognizing the diversity of learners, reducing barriers to learning, and addressing students' different needs right from the start. In any class, students will represent a heterogeneous mix of abilities, backgrounds, and learning styles. Some may have specific learning, physical, or sensory disabilities. They'll probably have diverse reading abilities. In universally designed classrooms, teachers aim to give all students access to the same high-quality content and to ensure that they meet similar learning goals. They use a variety of techniques and strategies to do so, however, and provide students with choices in how to achieve those learning goals.

What are some specific strategies used in a UDL classroom?

The goal of a UDL classroom is maximizing options—both for students and teachers—in order to enable students to learn content and skills in the most effective way. Teachers don't limit their presentations to lectures and printed materials, since these will not engage all students or be accessible to all. They might use concept maps or graphics to enhance and illustrate concepts. Students might be encouraged to use alternate means for note-taking, such as audio recordings, depending on what works best for them.

Assessment in a UDL-based class is a process rather than a single summative test—a way to identify what students are learning and to adjust instruction to meet each student's needs. Students demonstrate what they know in multiple ways—for some, that may mean creating a diorama or writing a story. A UDL classroom might have cooperative groups in which students take on different roles, share resources, and support each other's learning. These are just a few examples of UDL classroom strategies.

It sounds like UDL is just good teaching. Is there more?

Good teachers do many of these things routinely, so UDL in practice looks like good teaching at its best. But UDL provides a framework that makes explicit what good teaching is. It helps teachers recognize the diversity of their classrooms—because even those that might appear to be homogeneous are not. It helps them be explicit about the goals of the lessons and enables them to offer choices and alternatives for students to reach those goals.

How will UDL work with other curriculum programs we're already using in our school?

UDL usually complements other approaches, such as Differentiated Instruction or Understanding by Design. Of course, one of the concerns teachers often have—I worried about it when I was a teacher—is what the new "flavor of the year" will be. What new program will a district want this year? Because it emphasizes developing flexible learning environments through multiple means, UDL creates a framework that other district initiatives can hang from.

In the literature on UDL, there is a big emphasis on computer-supported learning. Does UDL require computers?

New technologies are an important tool for effective UDL implementation because of the incredible flexibility they give teachers in presenting and accessing material in diverse ways. This does not mean that the principles of UDL—to provide students with multiple representations of information, multiple ways to approach and engage in learning tasks, and multiple means to express themselves—cannot be applied in a classroom without technology. They can.

The media and materials we choose make a huge difference. What technology promises, though, is the ability to offer customized, individualized curriculum in ways that can be taken to scale. Students need both physical and cognitive access to the curriculum. Students with low vision can physically access the curriculum through digital text-to-speech, refreshable braille, and other innovations. A student with cerebral palsy, for example, can use a chin switch and other tools to write a response to a text, allowing appropriate assessments. However, for some students, the exclusive use of print inhibits cognitive access. For example, a student with a learning disability may be able to see the text clearly, but because of the disability may struggle to identify the main points in a text and needs prompts and model answers to scaffold understanding. He or she may be easily distracted without immediate background knowledge and vocabulary help—something a technological tool can offer without requiring the child to leave his or her seat. Highlighting and underlining tools might also help that student stay on track and digest the text. Even in a class of twenty, providing individualized learning support is a daunting task. The UDL-based technology solutions we are exploring at CAST incorporate research-proven teaching methods in digital learning environments.

Can you give an example?

The digital Thinking Readers—full-text computerized editions of middle-school novels like *The Giver* and *Tuck Everlasting* have built-in supports based on reciprocal teaching, an approach to reading comprehension instruction that two decades of research has shown to be effective. The Thinking Reader novels include reading-strategy prompts, model answers, background knowledge, and vocabulary support. All of these can be accessed and responded to in multiple ways, depending on what students need. For example, students with a learning disability such as dyslexia may benefit from text-to-speech, and synchronized highlighting features can help an English-language learner track words on a page and associate the way a word looks with the way it sounds—an enhancement that fixed materials, such as printed text, cannot provide. Those same features can also help students who do not have learning disabilities but may need extra support—English-language learners, for example—and the text-to-speech will also benefit students with low vision. The programs capture all kinds of just-in-time data on each student for progress monitoring. These are powerful supports for teachers and students that technology makes possible in a busy classroom setting.

Some children in my classroom use assistive technologies, like braille. Is UDL intended to replace these kinds of assistive technologies?

Teachers tend to confuse the two. As an approach, UDL is compatible with assistive technology, not in competition with it. There will always be a need for assistive technology. In fact, Universal Design for Learning grew out of CAST's research and development of assistive technologies. We realized at one point that assistive technology placed an emphasis on fixing the student—retrofitting the child to accommodate inaccessible curriculum. With UDL, we shifted our focus to fixing the curriculum. Our interpretation of the problem was that the curriculum is broken, not the child, and it needs to be designed in a way that accommodates the greatest number of students. It needs to be universally designed in the same way that universally designed buildings accommodate people with diverse physical abilities.

We have a lot of students who are not identified as special needs—some who are high achievers and others who struggle to learn. What does UDL offer them?

One of the things UDL points out is that we all have special needs, talents, and strengths. We all struggle to learn in some ways. There is enormous diversity among us in spite of the fact that some individuals have a label attached to them.

As individuals, we all struggle with different things or make choices according to what suits us best. In our trainings, teachers do an exercise in which they brainstorm the ways they would learn to cook an Indian meal. Suddenly you see people demonstrating widely different styles, preferences, and needs. Some say "Don't make me read the directions. I want to experiment." Others want an exact recipe to follow. The *a-ha* moment comes soon after as the members of the group realize that we all are different—our students, too. Some of us work best in digital environments and need the supports they have, whereas others do fine with "old-fashioned" texts.

UDL offers a way to extend beyond categories of disability to think about all of us as unique individuals. Because of the nature of our educational system, UDL tends to be placed in the special education category. But in fact, UDL is really a merging of general education and special education, a sharing of responsibility, resources, and ownership. It gets away from the "their kids–our kids" divide between general ed and special ed.

How does UDL apply to assessment?

Test results often say as much about the medium of the test—usually paper and pencil—and its limitations as they do about what students really know. UDL supports ongoing, formative assessments that inform instruction as it is happening, so teachers can intervene in a timely way. If the point is to assess skill learning in deeper, more meaningful ways, then students should have various means of expressing what they learn. This might mean having the option of writing or speaking final reports, creating an animation or video, or crafting a story in graphic form. For example, in Thinking Reader, students can accumulate a whole portfolio of responses to the embedded strategy prompts and questions, journal entries, audio-recorded reactions to the text, and more. Again, technology makes it easier for a teacher to provide every student with multiple options for expression. This gives a teacher a lot to work with in terms of helping that individual understand a text. On a broader scale, CAST is conducting very promising research on universally designed large-scale assessments. For example, one project looks at giving students with learning disabilities access to computer-based tests that let us focus on finding out what content students have actually learned rather than on whether they can work in a cumbersome medium—printed text.

REFERENCES

Rose, D. H., & Meyer, A. (2002). *Teaching every student in the digital age*. Alexandria, VA: ASCD.

Rose, D. H., Meyer, A., & Hitchcock, C. (2005). *The universally designed classroom: Accessible curriculum and digital technologies*. Cambridge, MA: Harvard Education Press.

Meyer, A., & Rose, D. H. (1998). *Learning to read in the computer age*. Cambridge, MA: Brookline Books.

CHAPTER FOUR

A Level Playing Field: UDL in the Classroom

LANI HARAC

Kelly Driscoll's humanities class wasn't nearly as rowdy as the group next door, but it was far from quiet. A computer-generated voice occasionally penetrated the muted clickety-clack of nineteen middle schoolers working on laptops, and a handful of kids tossed play-insults at each other between discussions of what they were reading.

Punctuating the buzz were intermittent pronouncements from a corner of the room. "Yessss!" Anais Perez exclaimed, setting her gold nameplate earrings swinging. "That's so sad," she said a few minutes later. Then, with conviction and a strong New England accent, "Such a liuh."

Her thick black hair wrapped in a messy bun, Anais and her classmates were using software called Thinking Reader to read *Bud, Not Buddy*, Christopher Paul Curtis's tale of an orphan's childhood during the Great Depression. Though the tone of the book is light, Bud's life in Flint, Michigan, is hard, with stints in cruel foster homes. As the class wrapped up on a morning in late May, Anais got into an exchange with Michael Guerra, a lanky boy seated across from her, about what happens during Bud's first night with a new family, the Amoses. Their son, Todd, makes a habit of harassing foster kids with a pencil, and Bud is no exception—although he's the one who gets punished by Todd's mother after the two boys are caught fighting.

"It's nasty, sticking a pencil up someone's nose," Anais observed. "I'd wanna go back to the [orphanage]. She didn't even hear Bud's side of the story."

"Would you believe your own kid or someone you found on the street?" Michael countered.

"You can believe both of them," Anais replied. "Sometimes you don't know who's telling the truth."

When Anais arrived at Young Achievers Science and Mathematics Pilot School (YA) as a second grader, she could barely read and she was performing below grade level in all of her classes at the K–8 school. The next year, she was given an individualized education plan (IEP), which until sixth grade meant that she left her classroom for large chunks of time to get extra help in reading, writing, and other subjects. When she was with her regular teachers, she usually tried to avoid reading altogether by misbehaving.

As one of Driscoll's seventh graders, however, Anais did something different this past year: she stayed in class. "I had a chance to sit . . . with kids my age, kids that are supposed to be in my grade," she says. "And that's instead of getting kicked out of the class."

Driscoll is a practitioner of something called Universal Design for Learning, born twenty years ago at a clinic not far from Young Achievers. The UDL approach—in which students use whatever print or technological tools they need—was originally devised for kids with physical and learning disabilities. It has been so successful among those students that the group responsible for it recently drew up guidelines for the federal Individuals with Disabilities Education Act (IDEA), currently up for reauthorization.

That same group, a nonprofit called the Center for Applied Special Technology (CAST), is now trying to get UDL into mainstream classes. Its researchers claim that with the right materials, technology, and training, teachers can make all lessons flexible enough to benefit every student—including those considered "disabled."

"We don't know any teachers who really want it the way it is, having school largely be a sieve separating students," says David Rose, a CAST founder. "It's no fun going home at the end of the day knowing you have students falling further behind while you do your job."

That may be true. But UDL, like any technology-related education-al approach, isn't cheap. And at least initially, it requires teachers to spend extra hours crafting lessons. So as the federal government and several state-level administrations add UDL to their education policies, it's worth taking a look at how it's applied in the Boston area, where CAST's wide-ranging theories have already met the day-to-day realities of the classroom.

Anais lives in Dorchester, a working-class Boston neighborhood, with her mother, three brothers, and a foster brother. They reside in a new single-family home on a street otherwise dotted with dilapidated apart-ment buildings. Her mother, Ana Dominguez, is a native of the Domini-can Republic who moved to Dorchester when she was fourteen, the age Anais is now. The thirty-four-year-old Dominguez bears a striking re-semblance to her daughter. She's a single mother who works part-time as an administrative assistant in a nursing home. Tall and broad-shoul-dered, Anais moves gracefully; until recently, she studied hip hop, bal-let, and tap at a dance school near Young Achievers, in Jamaica Plain. She spends most of her free time now hanging out with cousins who live close by.

Anais has always had academic problems, however. The Boston school district diagnosed her with something referred to as a "specific learning disability," although it's anything but specific. For Anais, it's exceeding-ly hard to identify words and figure out their meanings—"decoding," as literacy specialists call it. This means she has a tough time understanding written and spoken language and, therefore, struggles in all subjects.

Young Achievers is part of a network of "pilot" schools in the Boston area that essentially function as district-led charters and allow for in-novation. In grades 3–6, Anais's special ed teachers used a phonics pro-gram that helped her read stories like *The Cat in the Hat* on her own, although she was never able to keep up with classmates. By sixth grade, though, the routine had become unbearable, according to Anais. She was being pulled out of the classroom most of the day. "In the morning, I'd have to go into class for like two minutes," she recalls, "and then leave for two or three hours."

Things were different with Ms. Driscoll, a vibrant, down-to-earth twenty-nine-year-old with long brown hair often tucked behind her ears.

She was using Thinking Reader as part of a UDL-based curriculum that included everything from giving kids Post-its and highlighters for note-taking to establishing a library of books on cassette tape. When Anais used the software this past fall, she was able to finish a grade-level novel for the first time. Then, she says, "I read a whole book on vacation"—accompanied by a recorded version borrowed from Driscoll.

From a distance, UDL looks like many other technology-driven in-structional theories. But a few details set it apart. It was developed long before technology played such a prominent role in education; its cre-ators at CAST are among the genre's pioneers. UDL also allows teachers to make use of multiple pedagogical approaches and technological tools within a single curriculum. Most important, however, is an emphasis on across-the-board cooperation—involving not only CAST and teachers, but publishers, too, so that materials can be modified easily to suit indi-vidual students' needs.

Thinking Reader is a good example of how UDL works. When Anais used it for *Bud, Not Buddy* in May, she began at Level 1, the first of four. Passages were highlighted onscreen while recordings of the same text played aloud, enabling Anais to follow along, sometimes repeating words to herself. At intervals, the recording halted and the screen dis-played a prompt or exercise, such as "Look at the highlighted words in the text to help you visualize what is happening, then describe what you see in your mind." As Anais became more skilled, the number of support prompts decreased and they became less explicit. By June, when school was about to end, she'd moved up to Level 2.

"A student like Anais, who just struggles so much with reversals and what she sees—has she improved in her decoding?" Driscoll asks. "I would say yes, but her improvement in decoding is because she loves to read now. Reading is not as frustrating for her, and it's something she sees as a part of her life now. She is a student who has become, over the course of the year, confident in her learning."

Driscoll was teaching reading, writing, and social studies to seventh and eighth graders at Young Achievers. Of the nineteen students in her seventh-grade class, eight had IEPs. A few, including Anais, were Latino; the rest were African American. The walls of her classroom were cov-ered with posters on which Driscoll had used multicolored markers to write vocabulary words and reading comprehension strategies. During one lesson, she used an overhead projector to display atrociously punctuated sentences on a large screen. She would ask one student to correct each sentence—and, if necessary, call on classmates for help.

Driscoll began her career in 1998 in her home state of Connecticut, where she was a special ed teacher for three years. She moved to Boston in 2001, worked at a middle school that closed the following summer, then switched to YA. In summer 2003, she and a few other YA teachers attended a nearby workshop organized by CAST. Instructors there described one of their classroom programs—through which CAST helps educators hone lesson plans—and asked some of the teachers whether they wanted to participate. Driscoll considered the decision a "no-brainer."

"I like challenges, I like figuring out how people learn," she explains. "When you're an education student, you're asked to write about your philosophy of education. And the more I studied special education, the more I realized all education should be special education."

Special ed was actually the starting point for CAST. In the early 1980s, a group of clinical neuropsychologists at North Shore Children's Hospital in Boston were working with kids who had significant cognitive and physical disabilities. A few members of the staff, including David Rose, believed that the usual educational recommendations for these students were insufficient, so they began meeting separately to discuss alternatives and explore the ways computers might help.

In 1984, five of them founded CAST as an independent clinic. Children and their parents would visit the office, where the neuropsychologists frequently employed assistive technologies such as computers that recognize voice commands. "With the computer stuff, there were times when it happened right in front of us," recalls Rose, one of CAST's two directors and a former preK–12 teacher. "You'd see a kid who was disabled, and within a day, there was a huge change in what they accomplished."

Recreating the same environment in schools, however, was difficult. So in the mid-1990s, CAST's mission evolved from "fixing the child" to fixing the education system for students with disabilities. At the same time, Rose and his colleagues were doing extensive research that led them to develop a model of three brain networks central to the learning process. They argued that lessons should be "universally designed," accounting for these networks and their associated strengths and weaknesses in each student.

From this model, the CAST researchers concluded that "learning disabilities" had nothing to do with how smart kids are or how much they can achieve; what was disabled was the classroom material—only a narrow band of students could use it. A more flexible curriculum, they argued, would be accessible to everyone.

"We realized we could continue helping one child at a time, forever, or we could help a larger number of students," recalls Grace Meo, another CAST founder and currently its professional development director. "What we're doing is shifting the burden of change from the students to the curriculum."

Some Boston-area schools, in fact, have gone beyond even curricular changes, transforming their entire learning environments with accessibility in mind.

The four-year-old building that houses Ipswich Middle School, located thirty miles northeast of Boston in a town of the same name, was designed to be technology friendly. Every classroom has a half-dozen computers, and each grade level is clustered around what looks like a hexagonal conversation pit outfitted with high-tech multimedia equipment. The Ipswich district also provides free technology training to employees; Pat Previte, who's spent her seventeen-year career at the middle school, has taken part every summer.

Previte's sixth-grade English classroom is roomy and quiet, with several windows and a wall of cupboards. Although none of the eighty-five students in her four classes this past spring had an IEP, she worked with CAST curriculum designer Patti Ganley to create universally designed lessons. Since the mid-1990s, CAST has been designing "digital books" that offer oral and visual versions of texts and allow students to type, record, or scan in notations. (Print copies are available for students who prefer them.) Thinking Reader itself is a result of CAST's research. Now produced and distributed by Tom Snyder Productions, an educational software company based near Boston, the program is available even to teachers who aren't familiar with UDL. CAST has also prototyped and sold a number of other digital materials modeled on UDL principles, including the literacy software WiggleWorks and the Web accessibility tool Bobby, which determines whether Internet sites are disability friendly.

Previte didn't use Thinking Reader this past year, but she and Ganley developed their own digitized novel and allowed students to post comments on the class Web site as they read chapters. The last project of the year was a "teaching book," an idea Previte's daughter, also an educator, had fashioned with her own colleagues. Students could pick any topic and then, using Internet and print sources, put together their own books, becoming "experts" on their areas of study. As they made their presentations in the last week of May, Alex Buchbaum, a stocky boy with ruddy cheeks, authoritatively answered questions about military history without once referring to his spiral-bound book. Eli Natti, a charismatic student with shaggy brown hair and a slight lisp, enthused about violins: "If you weren't in Italy," he avowed, "you weren't a violinmaker. It's just that simple."

"The goal was to have the students recognize different types of non-fiction structures, and then [have them] take that and show they understand the text structures," Previte explains. "I was definitely able to see gains that they had made. I helped one boy but he did a lot of it himself, more than I think he has in the past."

The equipment needed to do these kinds of projects is expensive. Although final numbers for 2003–04 weren't available at press time, the market research firm Quality Education Data estimated that during the school year U.S. public schools would spend as much as $5.8 billion on educational technology. And this past spring, the Consortium for School Networking conducted case studies across the country, taking into account costs for maintenance, staff development, and other expenses. It found that each instructional computer had cost the districts between $1,000 and $3,000.

These are the kinds of numbers that concern Todd Oppenheimer. Winner of a National Magazine Award and author of the book *The Flickering Mind: The False Promise of Technology in the Classroom and How Learning Can Be Saved*, he argues that most of the money for technology is being spent ineffectively and could be better applied to the basics. But he does allow for what's called "scaffolding"—using computers to support kids rather than think for them. Text-to-speech software, for example, could read aloud an algebraic word problem to a dyslexic student, so long as that student then does the math herself. Although Oppenheimer hasn't had direct experience with UDL, he's encouraged by what he hears.

"You want to use the computer's powers to break down the steps of learning . . . to make them more complex, so you really engage [students] and hook them—and eventually get them off the computer," he says. "[UDL] certainly sounds promising. As long as it's not overused and oversold, I think this is one of the areas where computers have great promise."

Oppenheimer isn't alone in his assessment. Several states throughout the country have adopted UDL as an integral part of their education policies. And CAST was one of the primary collaborators on the National Instructional Materials Accessibility Standard (NIMAS), a voluntary set of guidelines for publishers who produce digital versions of materials for students with disabilities. NIMAS has been endorsed by the U.S. Department of Education and included in the 2004 Individuals with Disabilities Education Improvement Act.

"We used to think [our mission] was a line of code in the software; now we see it as a line of code in a bill," David Rose says. "What we're trying to do is build more power into the materials, and more flexibility, so the teacher doesn't have to remake it."

In June, Driscoll's seventh-grade classroom was awash with students getting ready to showcase final presentations for *Bud, Not Buddy*. Anais and two friends, Shardee Burston and Lynnicia Barnett, had decided to perform the scene in which Todd sticks a pencil up Bud's nose while he's asleep. After Bud awakens, he fights back—until Mrs. Amos enters and accuses him of picking on her son.

The students introduced the chapter, then Anais, in the role of Bud, curled atop a small table serving as a bed. Shardee, playing Todd, entered with a pencil in hand. The girls wrestled to the floor, then remembered to dip into a plateful of red paint. Both of them now smeared with "blood," Shardee held her neck as Anais ducked under the bed. Enter Lynnicia as Mrs. Amos, who listened sympathetically to Todd's version of events:

Todd: I was only trying to help, and . . . and look what it's gotten me.

Mrs. Amos (to Bud): This is how you choose to repay me? Not only have you struck him, you provoked his asthma!

Todd: I was just trying to wake him to make sure he'd gone to the lavatory. I was just trying to help.

Mrs. Amos (to Bud): Go to Todd and apologize, or I shall be forced to give you the strapping of your life.

Bud: It was wrong of me to hit you. I know you were only trying to help, and I'm very sorry for what I did.

The girls recited straight from the book, skipping a few lines here and there to keep the program short. What was notable, at least for Driscoll, was that Anais spoke publicly at all.

"It's incredible that she read out loud for her presentation because before, she wouldn't do that," Driscoll says. "We have had situations this year where teachers asked her to read out loud and then put consequences on her when she didn't do it."

At home that afternoon, Anais's mother, Ana Dominguez, admitted that she still has to prod the teenager to read. "But," she continued, "she says that she's doing better, that she's learning, that she feels more special."

Dominguez was sitting on a love seat in a tiny living room dominated by a large-screen television. Soon, Anais and her oldest brother, Michael, arrived. After a quick trip upstairs to her room, Anais dropped onto the couch next to her mom. "Wow," Dominguez said, looking at two small trophies in her daughter's hands. "*¿Dónde* Mikey?"

"He's upstairs. He only got one," Anais declared, showing off her soccer awards and a swimming certificate. She told her mother about the presentations in Driscoll's class and added that one of the observing teachers gave her group top scores in all grading areas.

Reflecting on the school year about to end, Anais recalled that in the fall, she kept waiting for someone to pull her out of class, as they had for years. It took her a few days to realize that with help from Driscoll and UDL, the pattern had changed.

"Now if I read a book, I'll understand it," she said. "It showed me . . . that reading isn't all that hard and that you can see your own work if you talk to the text and you think through your work. I'm not only at Level 1. I can go up to a Level 2, and a Level 3, and a Level 4."

CHAPTER FIVE

Teacher Perspectives: UDL in the Elementary Classroom

KIRSTEN LEE HOWARD

I recently saw an advertisement that said, "How can you hold thirty hands when you only have two?" It reminded me of Lev Vygotsky's theory of the Zone of Proximal Development, which I learned about while reading his book, *Thought and Language*, in my education classes. I connected immediately with Vygotsky's idea that each individual has his or her own unique learning zone; I liked the way this theory seeks to teach students in their own individual zones. For learning to take place, the material must be challenging enough to engage students' interest, but not so challenging that they become frustrated and give up. My challenge was to figure out how to make this teaching method a reality in my classroom of twenty-one diverse first graders with many different learning styles. How could I figure out how to make the curriculum accessible to each student? How could I implement Vygotsky's theory of twenty-one individual zones of proximal development? The answer for me was Universal Design for Learning (UDL).

FUNDAMENTALS OF UDL

I learned the fundamentals of UDL at a professional development institute offered by the Center for Applied Special Technology (CAST), a nonprofit educational research organization located in Wakefield, MA.

CAST developed UDL as an approach to teaching, learning, and assessment. UDL focuses educators on developing flexible curricula that provide students with multiple ways of accessing content, multiple means for expressing what they learn, and multiple pathways for engaging their interest and motivation. This approach allows teachers a multidimensional view of their students as learners, and offers them unique insights as they assess students' knowledge, interest, and understanding. Although UDL is by no means a simple way of thinking about and planning curriculum, I try to begin each planning session with a few simple questions:

- What is the basic idea that the students need to learn?
- What are different ways to learn this idea: demonstration? games? shared experience?
- If there is reading involved, do students have to read it by themselves, or can they use other tools and strategies to get the information?

I think about assessment in the same way:

- Is a test the best way to find out whether students learned the information?
- In what different ways can students demonstrate their understanding?
- Which will be meaningful for them?

UDL aims to provide each student with access to the curriculum in a way that promotes the most learning for that individual. Most educators wish to teach every student in the way that allows the optimum access to learning; I am always looking for ways to make this happen in my classroom. CAST invited me to share a few successes I have had in the hopes that what has worked for me can help inspire ideas that will work in other classrooms.

MY FIRST-GRADE CLASSROOM

The design of a first-grade classroom must take into account the most pressing challenges facing its students. I wanted to use the lens of UDL to address skill imbalance and attention span difficulties. My first graders have plenty of ability to comprehend text and ideas, but not all of them have the skills to decode at as high a level as they can comprehend. I have found that there is a dangerous tendency, especially when teaching struggling readers, to focus only on decoding skills and conduct most instruction using simple text. Selecting learning materials solely on the basis of students' decoding ability rather than considering their ability to comprehend the content can create an imbalance in students' reading skills as they get older.

Another thing I needed to keep in mind was my first graders' limited attention spans. They need engaging and interesting content provided in a flexible curriculum. They need the chance to ask questions, notice, and observe in a hands-on environment. If they lack these essentials, their motivation to learn often drops off.

With these challenges in mind, I changed my instructional practice to reflect UDL principles, and I integrated technology into our guided reading time. Combining the principles of UDL and computer technology with my assessment of what each student needed to help them learn yielded some results that I think Vygotsky would be proud of.

UDL IN PRACTICE

Part of our first-grade curriculum is an exploration of the needs of living things. We begin this study by learning about the needs of seeds and plants. Some wonderful children's literature is available on this subject. It occurred to me that I ought to try to integrate the reading of science material into our literacy teaching. Typically, much of our science reading takes place during science time and comes in the form of read-alouds. I have shied away from reading science content material during guided reading time in the past because it is often very difficult for many of my students to decode. I thought it would be interesting to approach this issue from a UDL perspective: figuring out how to break the decoding barrier as well as provide the students with appropriate supports to focus on the content.

I chose four books at different reading levels: *I'm a Seed*, by Jean Marzollo; *Growing Vegetable Soup*, by Lois Ehlert; *Diary of a Sunflower*, by Carol Pugliano; and *How a Seed Grows*, by Helene J. Jordan.

I placed the books at four stations around the classroom. I told students they would be reading one of these books at guided reading time the next day, but I wanted their help in deciding who would read each book. Students had about five minutes at each station to look through each book. Their job was to think about how well they could read it by themselves, whether it interested them, and if they would learn something new from the book. Students then ranked the books from their first through fourth choice. I told them I would look at their choices, try to give all students their first or second choice, and assign books to students for the following day. My task seemed clear: in assigning the students to the different books, I needed to figure out how to let each access his or her first choice, and whether it was a book he or she could decode independently.

Some of these decisions were simple: I assigned several students to their first choice, knowing that they would be able to read it independently. Other students I put into pairs. I knew that their reading skills would complement each other and that they would be able to decode and comprehend the book well together. For those students, I had enabled access to the content in their Zone of Proximal Development (ZPD) by selecting one child who would scaffold the other's reading, a key component of Vygotsky's ZPD theory.

I also provided technology-based scaffolds for struggling readers. For some, I recorded each book on a cassette tape, reading slowly and encouraging the readers to follow along with their fingers. I also stopped every few pages with questions for them to think about or important points for them to notice. The books chosen by a few of my students on individual education plans (IEPs) required the most preparation. One student has a documented print-based disability, and a few students needed more intense scaffolds than those provided in the audiotaped book. Using a scanner, I created computer-image files of the book's pictures. Next, I typed the text for each page into Dreamweaver, a software program for creating Web pages. I chose to use this type of program because it would allow me to "link" the pages together and students could navigate forward and backward through this program, just like a book. My school owns a copy of Dreamweaver, so I used this software, although many others are available. I imported the picture that I'd scanned previously into each page, creating a webpage that was very similar to the corresponding page in the book. I then linked the pages together. (This digitizing of school-owned copyrighted material is permissible when used for instruction of students with special needs as long as the digitized copy identifies the copyright owner, includes the original date of publication, and contains a notice that further reproduction may infringe on the copyright owner's rights.) I then opened this new document using the CAST eReader (now called AspireReader), a software program that reads text out loud while highlighting the word or phrase that is being read. The end result was a virtual book for students to use on the computer. With this digitized book and eReader, students are able to read independently, either by highlighting unfamiliar words and having eReader read the words to them, or by having the entire page read to them and then trying it on their own.

The next day was the real test. Would multiple means of engagement make the difference? Would all of my students be able to answer the science questions posed to them? Would decoding problems cease to be a barrier to understanding the content? Had I truly "universally designed" the guided reading time?

At the beginning of our guided reading time, I posed two questions: (1) What do seeds need so they can grow? and (2) What do seeds grow into? Each question was written in a different color and posted in three spaces around the room. I gave children sticky notes to mark the places in their book where they found answers to those questions. I worked with the students reading digitized books, helping them to capture their answers. The sticky notes matched the color of the question, so an answer to a purple question was marked with a purple note, and a green question with a green note. I also asked students to write answers on the sticky notes when they had finished reading and to stick the notes on chart paper under the appropriate question. I encouraged the students to listen to and read their assigned book as many times as they wished.

I was amazed at the way the guided reading time turned out. All of my students were focused, engaged, and curious. It was a bit louder than I had anticipated, but all of the noise was purposeful. Students were discussing the questions with their partners, pointing out things that they noticed, and asking each other questions. During our wrap-up time, in which we shared what we learned from the books, students saw what their classmates were reading and learning. The students that I assigned to use the digitized book with eReader were able to find examples to support each of the questions and to participate in our discussion. They were using eReader to read aloud the words they did not know and then to read on their own. Many asked if they could read the other books the next day. Because I had provided multiple scaffolds for the books, students were able to read the other books when they wanted, either independently, with a partner, on audiotape, or on the computer.

I have only one computer in my classroom, so I need to be strategic in order to enable all students access to it. I solve this by assigning the computer to certain students when there are specific projects or work that the computer can support. The different software is available to everyone during our "free times" and "workshop times." I am very careful to make sure all students get turns using the computer and the various software tools in the beginning of the year, as well as throughout the year when we use new software. Students who need computer-based supports know that they will get chances to use the computer at other times during the day when they are not directed to use the computer during a particular time.

My reflection on the success of the guided reading time led me to a few conclusions. I was providing practice in both comprehension and decoding and integrating other learning content into a reading instruction time. Students were able to see that learning happens across all areas—it is not compartmentalized so that you only learn about science during science time. Students also seemed to be inspired by their investigation into the texts; they were continuing to find answers to the questions in other books about seeds at other times during the next few weeks. At the end of the unit, and even well into a different study, my first graders still retained the knowledge they had gained.

The preparation was time consuming, 3–5 hours. However, the time spent was well worth it, and I have everything ready for future use as well as for use by other teachers. There are many ways to reduce the time, such as inviting families or older students to read the books on tape or to scan in pictures and type in text. We teachers tend to be very creative in finding ways to get all of our tasks done!

Another benefit is that I am able to allow all students access to different types of support. When they get the chance to experience each of the tools, they begin to learn what works for them and what does not. Students want to be independent learners. Generally, if they do not need the support of an audiotape, they don't use it that often. Students who are consistently drawn to a particular tool are usually those who need it.

HOW UDL ADDRESSED THE ISSUES

The more ways I find to use UDL in the classroom, the more often I see my students' individual needs being addressed. Using a UDL model to plan instruction helps me address many of the issues present in a first-grade classroom.

During guided reading, I addressed skill imbalance by supporting my students in accessing content they could comprehend but not yet decode. This allowed them to develop their comprehension skills using engaging and meaningful content. The multilevel structure of the activity (allowing the students to choose from four books with different levels of scaffolding) provided them with the flexibility they needed to read the book they chose, to answer questions that would help them in their future science work, and to be invested in what they were doing because they were part of the planning process.

Reading books they chose and knowing that they had ways to get help on words they didn't know improved my students' attention spans greatly. My first graders also love Post-it® notes, so having the opportunity to use the notes to mark parts of the book made them want to find answers to the guiding questions.

As a first-grade teacher, I am blessed with brilliant students who have an insatiable, voracious thirst for learning. Many of my students pick up books that I consider too hard for them; they do this because they really want to read them. They know the work is hard, but they don't see it as a deterrent to their learning. Before my experiences with UDL and different software tools, I was unsure how to let them proceed. Now, with UDL as a viable tool, who am I to stand in their way?

CHAPTER SIX

Teacher Perspectives: Strategy Instruction Goes Digital

NICOLE STRANGMAN

"Digital texts gave me an opportunity to use technology to help students who might not be successful in another modality."
—*Teacher Pat Previte*

Michelle Winslow, fourth-grade teacher at Connery Middle School, Lynn, Massachusetts, and Pat Previte, sixth-grade teacher at Ipswich (Mass.) Middle School have a common vision for every student in their class: that of an engaged, strategic reader who can apply his or her reading skills across all areas of the curriculum. But when each student in the class brings different strengths, weaknesses, and interests to the classroom, achieving this vision can seem a daunting, arduous task.

Michelle and Pat are pioneers in the exploration of technology's potential to strengthen and facilitate reading comprehension instruction. As part of a federally funded research project spearheaded by CAST, the pair transformed their reading instruction by introducing universally designed, digital, supported texts into the classroom. In the following interview, these two exemplary teachers share their views on using digital text to support reading comprehension.

Describe your classrooms at the time you were participating in this research project.

Michelle: My classroom had roughly eighty-five students. A large percentage of them spoke second languages (for example, Khmer, which is Cambodian, and Spanish). So in terms of literacy, they struggled. Their reading ability wasn't high or even on grade level.

Pat: My four English classes had a total of ninety-two students. Students in our sixth grade are heterogeneously grouped for English. In one class, I had several special-needs students. Reading levels in this class (tested by the Gates-MacGinitie Reading Test) ranged from the second-grade level to the post-high school level. In my three other English classes, the range of reading abilities was also very diverse.

Tell me about the digital texts you were using.

Michelle: The Thinking Reader, which is what we were using, integrates the Reciprocal Teaching Method [a research-supported instructional model developed by Annemarie Palincsar and Ann Brown] into digital versions of children's literature. At certain points in a chapter, students would be prompted to apply a strategy—summarizing, predicting, questioning, clarifying, or visualizing—and write a summary of what they had just read; if necessary, there was an area that they could click on for help. In the initial program, a genie and a bird would pop up and give the students a little help on how to respond. These agents basically offered ideas on what makes a good summary, what is a good visualization, what does it mean to clarify. They would also give models and think alouds—examples of a good response. Students' responses were captured electronically in a work log. The digitized texts could also be read aloud using the text-to-speech tool.

Pat: These digital texts we were using also applied Universal Design for Learning. Universal Design for Learning is an approach that uses technology to make the curriculum more flexible and better able to meet the needs of a classroom made up of a diverse group of students. The texts offered different levels of support, depending upon a particular student's needs.

FIGURE 1   Example of a Supported Digital Text

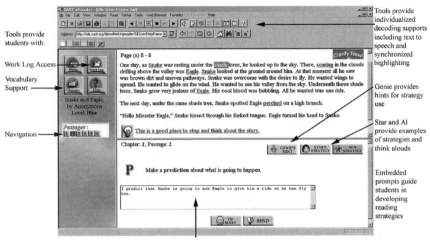

Work space for student responses that are sent to work log

What goals did you have for yourself when you decided to introduce these digital texts into your classroom?

Michelle: I feel that reading is of major importance. Reading difficulties have real consequences in all subject areas. If a student cannot comprehend the reading material, whether it is for math, science, or social studies, he or she will struggle. Also, my favorite subject is reading, and it's very interesting to me to realize that as a reader I already use many reciprocal teaching strategies without even realizing it. I summarize; I question. I wanted to learn how I could develop my students' repertoire of reading strat egies. Going to school to get my education degree, I learned a lot about the theory behind teaching and its development as a profession. But there were not many opportunities to learn a strategy-based approach, aside from certain situations that involved the study and development of curriculum around the theory of multiple intelligences. Reading strategies are not something that we even touched on.

Pat: Throughout my tenure as a middle-school English teacher, I have seen reading comprehension skills decline somewhat. Reading has always been of foremost importance to me as an English teacher, and its connection with the writing process is well documented. For the past decade, I have had access to computers in my classroom and have observed their effectiveness as a tool to support the writing process. I have become committed to the idea of using the computer and the Internet as a "library in a box" for the enhancement of reading and writing. Several years ago, working in conjunction with my principal, we tried unsuccessfully to acquire laptop computers for sixth graders. In September of 2000, however, providing each student with a laptop became a reality. We moved into a new building that housed two carts with fifteen laptops each, available for loan to interested teachers. Thinking Reader keyed into the library-in-a-box idea. One of its features is that it embeds in the text websites relevant to the theme of the novel that can enhance student background information. Thinking Reader also provided the impetus to use reading strategies to improve reading comprehension skills. It offered an opportunity to help all students improve reading comprehension skills by developing a reading program with embedded comprehension strategy prompts.

So all your students were reading on the computer?

Michelle: I had seven students, a mix of high-range, middle-range, and struggling readers, doing the majority of their reading on the computer. The rest of my students were in reading groups. They responded to the same prompts and strategies as students working on the computer, but they used the offline method of reciprocal teaching. They journaled their responses and took part in group discussions in which they would compare responses and/or seek clarifications.

Pat, your situation was somewhat different, right?

Pat: I've been using digital, supported texts for two years. In my case, all of the students work on the computer. Last year, we read Thinking Reader versions of *So Far from the Bamboo Grove* and *Number the Stars*. In addition to reading and discussing those novels, we read some articles about World War II that I found at EBSCO's Online Reader.

FIGURE 2   Two students independently discuss what they have been reading.

This year, we decided to expand on the one Holocaust novel that we did last year and do a whole unit on the Holocaust, using Thinking Reader versions of three novels: *A Traitor Among Us, Number the Stars*, and *Devil's Arithmetic*. We selected websites that would enhance the students' understanding of the European countries that were affected by the Holocaust. We didn't get too much into the thinking of Hitler or what happened in the concentration camps. We focused on the Resistance, doing extra reading on the Resistance movement. We also read a picture book on King Christian X of Denmark, *The Yellow Star*, to give the students background information on the King of Denmark, who is often referred to in *Number the Stars*. In addition, we did a play, *The Diary of Anne Frank*, to give students a realistic overview of what going into hiding was like. For a final project, we wrote poems that reflected students' thoughts on the Holocaust. To help students develop their thoughts on the Holocaust, I printed out their work logs for the Visualization and Feeling prompts for them to look at. In addition, CAST created a packet of many different styles of poems, such as "I Wonder" poems, bio poems, and shape poems.

Had your students done work on computers before?

Michelle: Not in the classroom, but they did have a computer lab that they went to, accompanied by our computer teacher. There they practiced basic software skills and learned to do various types of research using the Internet.

Pat: In the past, I've had them do research on the Internet and then present PowerPoint pieces. I've also had them adapt a research paper into a PowerPoint presentation, which was a better use of the two tools because when they weren't asked to do the research paper they often just copied what was on a website and reproduced it in the PowerPoint presentation. When they wrote the research paper, they used more of their own words. So, I learned a lesson from that! As I mentioned before, I have used computers in my classroom since 1996. I have made slideshows with picture clues to enhance vocabulary instruction, used picture prompts for writing ideas, and I have created PowerPoint shows to outline aspects of the different civilizations we study.

How did this use of digital texts differ from the way you approached reading instruction in the past?

Pat: This was different because instead of having the teacher use the technology to present some material, the students themselves were actively engaged with the technology. The digital texts gave me an opportunity to meld technology with my ability to help students who might not be successful in another modality [print versus speech]. For the first time, I could see into students' minds as they worked their way through the novels. Reading student work logs gave me amazing insight into what they understood about what they were reading and what they didn't. I realized that they had no knowledge of the Resistance movement and some basic aspects of the book important to its understanding. Our classroom discussions were more focused and took on a greater relevance to the development of reading comprehension.

Figure 3   A student responds to a strategy prompt while reading a digitized novel.

Michelle: Before, I would often discuss the elements of literature while engaging my students. I would touch upon various strategies that could be used to problem solve a difficult type of text, but I wouldn't link them as a unit.

In your experience, are there concrete benefits to using this kind of supported, digital text?

Michelle: In order to be successful we all need a plan. Strategy-based instruction gives students that plan—a tool that they can reach for and implement when they are struggling with something.

Pat: One benefit is that reciprocal teaching strategies help the readers get into the text and fine-tune their understanding. Also, because of the text-to-speech component, students who are stronger listeners than readers can move at a faster pace than they ever could have when reading the printed text. The strategies that are used and the constant written responses to the text improve students' writing skills.

Michelle, did you see any major differences in the impact of the reciprocal teaching approach on students working on and off the computer?

Michelle: It's one thing to accomplish these strategies on the computer and type in your responses. It's another thing to transfer it to the work you are doing outside. Sometimes I felt like the students reading on the computer were a whole separate entity. So I would try to bring them back to the reading groups and allow them the opportunity to respond and express their opinions. What I found was that their confidence, even in front of the entire group, had improved tremendously. There were no "surprises" for them, and they were able to think and analyze the way they were going to respond before engaging in the whole-group discussion of a particular chapter or passage. It was fun to see the online students' confidence soar and develop.

So there were some real changes in students' self-esteem?

Pat: I agree. I saw students talking to each other about what they had read, and that was a wonderful way of building their idea of, "Well, I'm a reader, too." Also, as far as the impact of the digitized text on students' self-esteem, many students were able to read one or two books in the time that they might have only been able to read half a book.

Michelle: One of my students was very withdrawn, very shy, and never raised her hand in class. Shortly after she started working with the digitized text she developed confidence. Through her involvement with the prompts and read-alouds, she knew that she would understand the question or the process of summarizing. Instead of trying to fade away into the background, she felt like "I know what I'm doing here!"

That's very interesting—you might expect that the students would struggle more with group discussion, having spent a lot more time by themselves.

Michelle: That's why I tried as much as possible to get them off the computer. Because they had so much assistance, a lot of them would finish ahead of the students who were reading offline. So I would have them bounce ideas off one another in the classroom library before returning to the whole group to discuss the passages that had been read that day.

How did the project impact students' reading comprehension?

Michelle: The students took a pre- and post-test [the Gates-MacGinitie Reading Tests], which focuses on vocabulary and comprehension. The students' scores were pretty low at the beginning, but by the end of the program they had improved. There were also end-of-novel assessments that allowed us to gather pertinent details regarding the students' overall comprehension of the important events and details of the story.

Pat: I think that using the digitized novels had a positive impact on students' reading comprehension. The work logs showed that they had to stop and think about what they read. They had a much better understanding of some nuances of the story than I think they would have had with a regular reading of the book. And reading the digitized novels really propelled many students who were borderline readers into a greater understanding.

Did this approach impact your ability to meet different students' needs?

Pat: Many boys are auditory learners. Auditory learners benefited a great deal from having the story read to them. One boy, in particular, said, "I can't read fast visually, but I can hear fast." So, I think that definitely helped not only his ability to be able to listen to and understand what he heard, but also to go through the text more quickly. In a more general sense, the digitized novels offer a very different approach to reading to a multitude of students who, even though they aren't struggling, are not what you would consider children who would easily sit down and pick up a book and read.

Michelle: This approach definitely helped me meet students' needs. Every student felt more confident, just by learning that there were strategies to enhance his or her reading comprehension. Students felt armed and ready to attack any form of text, because they had a "plan." Some students disliked some of the strategies, and you could see that in their responses, but all of them found something that they felt really comfortable with. For example, some of my students wanted to visualize all the time, because that was their area of strength. I think every single one of them felt like they were contributing.

They were all intrigued, and motivated to read or respond to text that they would not have even attempted before the program. The strategies were like a special recipe for success, effective for every student.

How did the students react when you introduced the computer work?

Michelle: It took time for them to adapt. At first, they showed some opposition to having to learn something new. Eventually, as they saw the fruits of their labor, they wanted to learn how to use the strategies better, and even went so far as to use them in other content areas. Also, there was some animosity because some students were spending a lot of time on the computer and others were not. But eventually they saw through their conversations with each other that the approach was truly helping to improve all of their reading abilities. At the end of the year, they were disappointed when they learned that their seventh-grade class wouldn't be participating in the same research project.

Was there anybody who really didn't like or benefit from the experience?

Pat: Yes. A couple students might have been better off if we'd given them, maybe, picture books, because I think the stories were too complex for them, given their attention spans and their motivational levels. They needed something that they could get through in a short time period, and there were too many multilayered characters for them. I think that if they had had something shorter, that it would probably have worked better for them. I think everybody else benefited greatly from it, though. Other students elected to read the book itself and not use the computer. However, only two or three students elected to read the book rather than listen to it read to them.

Michelle: A couple of kids just wanted to sit at their desks. They didn't want to get involved with the group. However, it wasn't long before the continued group interaction caused them to sit up and take part in all of the discussion that was taking place around them.

FIGURES 4–5 **Students in Michelle's class completed their unit on** *So Far from the Bamboo Grove* **by constructing murals.**

How about second-language learners?

Pat: I had an English-as-a-second-language student who increased his comprehension almost a grade level, because he really took to the listening. The faster pace with which he could listen proved very beneficial to him.

Michelle: I had one student who had come from Kenya. He was struggling in all academic areas. But over the course of this project, he slowly learned the usefulness of the strategies and, because of the repetitive nature in which it was used in the classroom, became familiar with the terminology. Having this approach strengthened his willingness to participate in discussions. He began to appear more confident in his written responses, and his strategy responses got longer. After this project, he loved working on the computer.

You have already mentioned a few ways that you assessed what students learned. Were there other assessment methods that you used?

Michelle: There were a variety of ways that I took stock of students' progress throughout the project. Periodically, I administered a chapter check-up that would focus on a particular passage. The students would follow along as I read the passage aloud, and then they would respond to each strategy. As often as possible I held miniconferences with the online students in which we would analyze their work logs and discuss their strengths in using the reading strategies as well as areas of concern. It was a great opportunity for both of us to touch base, reflect on the overall process, and get a true sense of how they were doing. They also took quizzes focusing on various strategies in a particular passage at various points throughout the book.

Pat: One way that I gauged how well kids were using the strategies and understanding what they were reading was to read their work logs. I got into their minds a little bit more than I would have if I hadn't had the work logs—and that was terrific.

Michelle: At the end of reading *So Far from the Bamboo Grove,* the class created a Book Mural. One group illustrated characters, a second group illustrated the various settings, a third group illustrated the prob-

FIGURES 6–8   Student Artwork from the Final Poetry Project

lems faced by the characters throughout the novel, and a fourth group illustrated the solutions that the characters devised to get through each devastating element of their journey (this section truly spoke of the resiliency, courage, and creativeness of the main characters). The mural provided the opportunity for a creative retelling of the novel and evaluated how well the students could focus on the critical events in the story.

The Book Mural seems like a great approach to avoid the problem of writing barriers preventing second-language learners from demonstrating what they learned.

Michelle: Yes, these students know that they have that barrier. And the group interaction around the mural allowed them the opportunity not only to share their thoughts and opinions, but also to gain any clarifications that they might have needed regarding the four elements of the novel.

Pat: For the poetry final project, my students also did illustrations to go with their poems. We began with an art lesson and gave students a choice of several different artistic media to work with: watercolor, charcoal, and Cray-Pas. As a model for the project I read several poems and showed artwork from the work "I Never Saw Another Butterfly," poems and drawings of children from the Terezin concentration camp. CAST took all the poems and drawings and created an anthology titled *Dark Horizons*. It contains an exemplary display of students' poetry and artwork.

Do you think this experience changed the way your students look at reading?

Michelle: The students loved the novels, and because of strategy-based instruction they were truly a part of the text in each one that they read. They loved it! I can bring up one of those novels six months from now and they'll still remember the specific events, details, characterizations, etc. But in a more general sense, the students suddenly became interested in chapter books that in the past they commonly passed over in favor of simpler, quick reads. And whereas they hadn't seemed interested in book orders, after a period of time with this project, they began to request that I pass them out. They would often seek my advice to determine what books would be of interest to them.

Pat: I think students not only understood but engaged with the text—the poetry and artwork they developed really illustrates that.

How about their writing?

Pat: There was a lot more detail in my students' explanatory writing than I've seen in the past. I was using a rubric to grade their work, and

I was giving, you know, A after A. That's very unusual. So, they did a very, very good job. They really did. And I thought that the poetry they wrote at the end of the unit came out very well. I think that they were a lot more confident in their writing because they had written up to six times a day in response to what they were reading.

Did you find the technology aspect of this project challenging?

Pat: I've always believed that technology is an instructional aid, so I found it easy to integrate the digitized novels into my teaching.

Michelle: Yes, at times I struggled with certain technical issues, but I learned many new approaches to solving them. I'd say that through this program I enhanced both my literary skills and my computer software skills.

Do you have any words for other teachers who might be interested in getting into reciprocal teaching or doing something on the computer?

Michelle: I strongly encourage educators at all levels to familiarize themselves with reciprocal teaching and its strategies. They will build up a tremendous repertoire of skills that can be shared with their students and that will allow for a broader approach to reading instruction. And the concept can be carried over into all academic disciplines.

CHAPTER SEVEN

Implications of Universal Design for Learning for Classroom Assessment

DAVID H. ROSE AND ROBERT P. DOLAN

I f you were a gardener and wanted to improve the yield of a tomato plant, you would assess the plant's health and growth during the growing season. You could then use the information to design interventions to improve the plant's yield. Using your assessment data, you would prune the plant to improve its structure and health. You would ensure that the plant presents all of its leaves to the sun to achieve optimal productivity. You might tie drooping stems to a stake, supporting them as they grow and preventing contact with the wet ground, where they can rot. You would reduce the number of side stems that detract from the growth and strength of main stems, thereby reducing the quality of fruit.

Assessments can be used to evaluate and support the performance of students, teachers, schools, school districts, and even materials and methods. The school district, for example, may conduct student assessments as an indirect measure of teacher performance, to analyze the effects of changing school practices, or to enable comparisons with other school districts, and students may conduct self-assessments as a way of identifying comparative strengths and weaknesses and needed areas of study.

In this article, we discuss some of the limitations of typical assessment practices and look at how applying Universal Design for Learning (UDL) principles can improve both assessment accuracy and its application to instruction. In particular, we consider assessments that directly address core issues such as monitoring progress, instructional intervention, and increasing motivation to achieve. However, the principles provided here also hold for other assessment applications, such as large-scale assessments.

LIMITATIONS OF ASSESSMENT ACCURACY

The value of an assessment as a means for informing instruction is a function of its accuracy. Accuracy, in turn, is a function of how well an assessment measures students' abilities vis-à-vis particular educational goals. An inaccurate assessment is one in which this information is confounded by other factors of student performance that are irrelevant to a particular learning goal.

Although there are remarkable individual differences among students, most existing methods of assessment were not designed with these individual differences in mind. In fact, many assessments appear to have been designed with the assumption that learners are relatively homogeneous and that relatively similar outcomes are expected for all students. As a result, assessments are rarely free of confounding information and thus rarely provide a truly accurate measure of student abilities.

We can use the principles of UDL to structure our examination of the accuracy of current assessment techniques, considering their ability to provide multiple means of representation, multiple means of expression, and multiple means of engagement.

Representation

Consider Patrick, a student with dyslexia. When he sits down with a standardized paper-and-pencil science test, he is likely to experience an all-too-familiar dread. The page full of text is daunting. Decoding the questions printed in the test booklet may pose difficulties for him that are as challenging as those posed by the science content itself. With many questions to read and a strict time limit, Patrick's science knowledge may be obscured by his problems reading the test. Moreover, many objective tests are purposely constructed with complex syntax and other linguistic structures so that the items provide greater differentiation among students. This means that, quite independent of their physics knowledge, students like Patrick and those with other language-based disabilities will achieve lower scores than those without such disabilities. Their scores will only partly reflect their knowledge of science.

The problem with science tests such as this is that they not only measure science knowledge, they also measure facility with the print medium. For Patrick, who is not facile with printed text, delivering the assessment in print depresses his score regardless of his science knowledge. Thus, in his case the test has poor accuracy.

Let's suppose that the teacher administered the test orally to the whole class. This would not necessarily make the test more accurate. There is in fact no single medium that would provide an unbiased vehicle for assessment. If a different medium, like oral language, were chosen to represent the science problems, Patrick's scores might improve, but at the expense of other students for whom speech poorly conveys the test material.

Because there is an inevitable interaction between the representational demands of the medium and students' individual capacities, there will be some inadvertent effect of the assessment medium for each student. For some, the effect is relatively negligible or even positive. For others, like Patrick, the effect is significant and negative. For any group of students, and particularly any group of diverse students, the fixed version of the test provides scores that are unreliable and distorted by the unseen weight of the medium. As a result, there is no single class-wide method for accurately assessing knowledge of science.

Expression

If the same standardized paper-and-pencil science test is handed to Daniel, a student with a physical disability, he will fail it outright due to his physical limitations. (He cannot hold a pencil.) So would many other students with physical disabilities—even a science expert such as Steven Hawking, the Nobel Prize-winning author and preeminent physics professor who has ALS (amyotrophic lateral sclerosis). In no case would failure purely reflect science knowledge because science knowledge would be confused with the ability to master the means of expression required by the paper-and-pencil test. While Daniel's case is extreme, easily demonstrating that the test cannot extract an accurate measure of science knowledge for everyone, it exemplifies the fact that a test that offers only a single mode of expression poses obstacles to accuracy just as does a test that offers only a single mode of representation.

The problem of expression is not restricted to extreme cases like Daniel's; the effects of tests such as these can be quite broad. Research is emerging that shows strong effects of the mode of expression on students with no obvious disabilities. For example, researchers at Boston College (Russell, 2000) have completed a set of studies investigating the role of different modes of expression (handwriting versus keyboarding) on the standardized test scores of general education students. Results indicate that student scores, which were supposedly based on test content alone, were sensitive to the response mode. That is, students who had experience on computers scored much higher on the test when they were able to keyboard than when they handwrote their response.

Engagement

Assessments can create special problems of engagement. Some nontrivial level of engagement is clearly required in order for an assessment to reflect optimal performance accurately. That is why assessment in school is usually associated with intensified emotions for students. Assessment is often the gateway to the most significant rewards and punishments. These external rewards and punishments take on a high level of affective significance—often fear or anxiety.

However, we know that there are tremendous individual differences in affective reactions to external rewards and punishments. This means that the same rewards and punishments will have very different motivational effects on different students. What is intended and even assumed to evoke the same level of motivation in everyone, can provoke a very uneven effect.

The critical difficulty is that there is an optimal level of engagement for any particular task and any particular assessment. Very low and very high levels of engagement tend not to support performance optimally on most tasks, but there are considerable differences in the results, depending on whether the task calls for creative thinking, divergent or convergent problem solving, or production of rapid, skillful solutions. We have all felt the disabling effects of anxiety—the metaphorical choking. There is no stable way to assess performance across different states of arousal. For example, the 90 percent foul shooter can be reduced to a 50 percent foul shooter by placing him or her at the line in the last seconds of a championship basketball game. On any task there is an optimal level of emotional arousal, and that level varies across individuals and settings (Goleman, 1995).

Applying external, fixed rewards that are the same for everybody will have highly differential effects on performance. While the rewards associated with testing and assessment are designed to raise the level of anxiety for every student—and thus, it is hoped, their performance—such rewards are likely to have a deleterious effect for a student who already experiences heightened anxiety. If a student's level of anxiety is chronically high, he or she is likely to be highly reactive to anxiety-producing events like testing. The affective significance the student attaches to the fear of failure may move him or her very far from an optimal level of arousal, resulting in poor test performance.

The particular affective state that any student attaches to assessment is dependent on his or her individual makeup and on the particular punishments and rewards. Because these factors differ greatly among individuals, the use of any single means of engagement will not accurately measure optimal performance for every student.

UNIVERSALLY DESIGNED ASSESSMENT

In light of student differences, it is clear that administering assessment in a common format does not level the playing field as many educators believe. Rather, a single format tilts the playing field, favoring some students and hampering others. The solution lies in providing a flexible test administration vehicle that provides students the opportunity to demonstrate their understanding and skills according to the particular learning goals associated with the assessment. In a universally designed curriculum, multiple means of representation, expression, and engagement are available as a normal part of every learning environment and every assessment.

Providing Multiple Means of Representation and Expression

A universally designed test allows some variation in the manner in which the test material is presented so that students are better able to express what they know. Thus, the test is more accessible. For example, presenting the test on the computer rather than solely in print provides many options for access. In Daniel's case, the computerized test allows him to take the test independently, using a single-switch access program or voice input—whereas in the print version, Daniel is denied access entirely.

For a wide range of other students who do not have physical disabilities, the representation and expression options in a universally designed assessment go beyond providing accessibility and serve to increase accuracy. We have already noted that the opportunity to type answers rather than write them on paper makes a huge difference for experienced computer users (Russell, 2000), illustrating that a test often confounds fluency with the response mode with knowledge or comprehension. For another example, voice-control options in a universally designed text would have a dramatic impact on other students, especially those with dysgraphia and dyslexia.

In the case of representation, UDL assessments could use multimedia to present material in ways that are tailored to the student's best medium for understanding. In this way, a student such as Patrick could understand what he is being asked without being punished for poor decoding ability. With respect to expression, imagine future UDL assessments in which verbal comprehension questions are complemented by or replaced with alternatives. For example, students might complete a drawing instead of a sentence to show the next step in a scientific process. More likely, students will be presented with virtual labs, where actual manipulations of data, technologies, or substances are used to demonstrate more clearly than any verbal response that the student understands the particular processes, methods, and outcomes—that they comprehend the science, not just the words. These options create a more interesting, more accurate, and often more relevant assessment of learning for a wide variety of students and a wide variety of subject areas. For example, with universally designed assessment it might be possible to determine that a student knows how to create a good summary pictorially or orally, even if he or she can't write one. That information provides a much clearer indication of the kinds of educational interventions that a particular student needs.

Providing Multiple Means of Engagement

One reason that traditional assessments are not very predictive of later success is that they rely too heavily on grades. As a means of engagement, grades may work for many students, but the effects are highly variable. For some students, the stakes are set too high by testing in general and grading in particular, leading to a lowered performance level often described as test anxiety. For others, the stakes are set too obliquely, so that grades are not a strong motivator.

It is important to emphasize the potential value of embedding assessment in the curriculum. Most free-standing tests isolate assessment, imbuing it with the character of an obstacle, hurdle, or failure detector. This eliminates the more positive role of assessment, that of providing an ongoing source of feedback. By incorporating assessment within the routine of interacting with material, it becomes active feedback that is found in any learning situation. This type of ongoing, formative evaluation is a critical part of learning, yet is rarely provided in school, replaced instead by summative evaluation.

In our science example, performance in only one content area is assessed. It is typical to assess science comprehension strategies using fixed, uniform, artificial content: every student receives the same passages, which are selected for their readability, syntactic complexity, and other criteria. These passages are not selected for their interest or relevance, or the level of engagement they stimulate. While this design may appear to ensure comparability among students, differences in levels of engagement interfere with this goal.

Imagine instead that the choice of content were flexible, made part of the universal design. For some students, this flexibility would have a very significant effect. They might be much more likely to produce a good summary of material that interests or engages them. A teacher would find it valuable to know that a student might be able to make an excellent summary of a comic book, but not a folktale. This student would require a very different type of intervention from a student who could not compose an adequate summary regardless of his or her level of engagement. Unless student assessment is conducted under optimal motivational conditions, unnecessary remediation may be the result.

USING UNIVERSALLY DESIGNED ASSESSMENT TO INFORM INSTRUCTION

The universally designed assessment has the ability to ensure that assessment instruments are both accessible and practical for students with disabilities. However, as we have argued here, the ultimate value of universally designed assessments goes far beyond access and practicality. UDL's inherent flexibility in representation, expression, and engagement can reduce the common sources of error introduced by fixed assessments, errors that interfere with accurate measurement of learning. That same flexibility allows teachers to align assessment more closely with teaching goals and methods, to vary those goals and methods, and to assess them accurately within the instructional venue. The future is even richer. The interactive capacity of new technologies allows the design of dynamic assessments that assess the ongoing processes of learning more organically. By tracking the particular supports a student uses, the kinds of actions and strategies that he or she follows, the actions and strategies that seem to be missing, and the aspects of the task environment that bias the student toward successful or unsuccessful approaches, these new assessments give teachers information that can significantly increase their understanding about the student as a learner.

A much richer set of options is available when the lesson itself becomes part of the assessment. Imagine that the teacher has set comprehension goals for students who need help in reading for meaning. Rather than wait until the end of the passage to assess students' comprehension, assessments could be embedded throughout the digital version of the chapter, displayed specifically for those students whose instructional goals make them appropriate or necessary.

These chapter-embedded comprehension checks would function less like the traditional test and more like scaffolds with feedback. They are more strategically useful to the reader, providing support for building meta-awareness and self-monitoring strategies relevant to comprehension. Expression of what the student knows and when he or she knows it becomes a normal part of interacting with text, rather than pass-fail information gathered at the conclusion of instruction, when performance is compromised by memory strain.

Most important, new technologies allow two-way interactive assessments. They enable the creation of learning environments that not only teach, but also learn. By distributing the intelligence between student and environment better, the teacher is able to learn about the student (e.g., his or her individual strengths, weaknesses, and styles) and keep track of the successes and failures of the curriculum. The result is a curriculum that becomes smarter, not more outdated, over time.

Finally, new technologies allow dynamic assessments to be universally designed. With a full range of customizations and adaptations as a part of assessment, student performance will be evaluated more accurately. This increased accuracy will result from evaluating performance under varying conditions, ranging from situations in which the student's performance is constrained by barriers inherent in available modes of representation, expression, or engagement, to situations where appropriate adaptations and supports are available to overcome those barriers.

An Example

To evaluate Patrick's progress in learning summarization strategies, his teacher can have him read a digital version of the content with an option for text-to-speech. This technique would enable the teacher to evaluate both Patrick's knowledge of science and his growth in summarization skills more accurately. Suppose, for example, that Patrick scored dramatically better on both the science and summarization questions with speech turned on. That would suggest that he has already learned how to summarize and comprehend adequately, and that his low scores without text-to-speech reflect primarily decoding difficulties, not difficulties related to summarization. In terms of strategic teaching, the teacher would know that it is necessary to concentrate on Patrick's fluency, rather than offering remedial instruction in summarizing strategies. The teacher might also decide that to enhance Patrick's learning of science, sound should be kept on whenever he is working independently.

This is only the tip of the diagnostic iceberg. The same flexibility can be applied to many other kinds of representation, in the form of vocabulary support, links to background information, syntactic support, and graphic organizers before, during, or after reading. Each of these scaffolds could be a regular part of a universally designed document. The flexibility to turn them on and off allows customization for the needs of each student, but also provides a mechanism for assessment: "Does vocabulary support help Patrick?" is an easy question to assess when the ability to turn it on and off is available. The key point is that a universally designed assessment instrument provides the flexibility needed not only to make it accessible, but also to make it more accurate and instructionally valuable. It does this by providing options: options that are essential to assess what is working and what is not.

SHORT-TERM SOLUTIONS FOR ASSESSMENT

Currently there are very few formal assessments that are universally designed and very few curricula that have embedded universally designed assessment. This limited availability will soon change. Publishers are already beginning to work on this project. Changes may happen relatively quickly due to public policy, intense economic incentive, and the availability of new technologies.

In the meantime, what can educators do? First, it is possible to modify existing methods of assessment so that they are more accessible and flexible. One straightforward step is to administer existing print-based tests on the computer. In that format, the test becomes much more flexible (e.g., the print can be enlarged, the text can be read aloud) and accessible to a variety of students. Many of the existing accommodations offered to students with disabilities who participate in large-scale tests can be provided in this way (IDEA Partnerships and the Council for Exceptional Children, 2000). This is an enormously helpful step, and one that is not difficult to take. For techniques and software tools that can make this step even easier, the CAST website (www.cast.org) provides relevant information and links to helpful resources.

Next, for any new or recent curriculum materials, ask publishers for accessible versions. By law, you are able to remake accessible versions. However, publishers are increasingly under pressure by many states to provide accessible versions of educational materials from the outset. In the years ahead, it is critical that educators and adoption committees ask publishers to provide materials that can be used by all students. More than anything else, consumer requests provide publishers with the incentive to do the right thing. As publishers become accustomed to meeting minimal standards for accessibility, they will learn to produce assessments that are truly universally designed. At that point, accurate assessment of all of our students will no longer be the sole responsibility of the classroom teacher, but will be an integral part of the education system.

REFERENCES

Goleman, D. (1995). *Emotional intelligence: Why it can matter more than IQ*. New York: Bantam.

IDEA Partnerships and the Council for Exceptional Children. (2000). *Making assessment accommodations: A toolkit for educators*. Reston, VA: The Council for Exceptional Children.

Russell, M. (2000). It's time to upgrade: Tests and administration procedures for the new millennium. *The Secretary's Conference on Education Technology 2000*. Washington, DC: U.S. Department of Education.

CHAPTER EIGHT

The Promise of New Learning Environments for Students with Disabilities

BART PISHA AND SKIP STAHL

AUTUMN IN MR. GUNDERSON'S HIGH SCHOOL CLASSROOM

At 9:45 a.m., twenty-eight chattering students file into Mr. Gunderson's high school U.S. History class. The room is bright and tidy. Mr. Gunderson is proud of the curriculum he has developed over his fifteen-year career. He has divided the six-pound history textbook into fourths, each corresponding to one of the academic calendar's quarters, and he has painstakingly drawn explicit connections among the text, his daily PowerPoint lecture presentations, the eighteen videos he uses each year, weekly quizzes, and quarterly hour-exams. Three computers with Internet connection are available to his students, but these are used only intermittently for carefully guided online resource explorations.

By all accounts, Gunderson is a dedicated and skilled professional. He knows his subject, he enjoys his students, and he does everything that he can think of to ensure that his kids are prepared for the state-mandated high stakes test each spring. Still, he is troubled by the 15 to 20 percent of his students who do not pass annually. He knows that the high stakes testing his state has adopted mandates serious consequences for failure, with potentially lifelong implications, whether the students realize it or not. He takes the task of teaching his five daily classes of diverse learners seriously, and is at his wit's end. How can anyone teach classes where many of the students speak a language other than English at home, where several have part-time jobs, and where TV, video games, and online chat rooms absorb up to thirty hours of students' time weekly?

The class sits down and the students drag out notebooks and pencils, anticipating Mr. Gunderson's opening remarks and an account of the fundamental underlying causes of the Whiskey Rebellion of 1794. The lesson is important for understanding U.S. history, since the rebellion marked the first time under the new Constitution that the federal government had used military force to exert its authority to regulate commerce. Eric takes a seat in the front of the room, prearranged for him as an adaptation to help him compensate for his medically diagnosed Attention Deficit Hyperactivity Disorder (ADHD). Mr. Gunderson paces back and forth in front of him, showing the passion with which he approaches both history and teaching. Eric's attention follows Mr. Gunderson, who sketches a map and several bushels of corn on the chalkboard. Dutifully, Eric copies the names of key players and dates of key events into his tattered notebook.

Sun streams in through the window, steadily warming the room to an uncomfortable temperature. Eric's pencil vaults from his grasp, landing on the desktop. He rolls the wayward pencil forward and back, then spins it like a compass needle, hoping to predict where the pencil will point when it comes to rest.

His concentration is interrupted by a query from Mr. Gunderson, "Eric, were the Pennsylvania farmers right or wrong to object to the whiskey tax imposed on them in 1791?"

Eric responds, "Yes, absolutely!" and is rewarded by gales of laughter from the class. It's better to be a clown than to be viewed by friends as stupid.

Seated two rows from Eric, Ellen pays as little attention as possible to him. She has no patience with class clowns, who threaten to distract her from the lecture. She is concentrating on Mr. Gunderson and scribbling furiously in her notebook, struggling to capture every fact, every name, and every date that might appear on a test. Unlike Eric's notebook, Ellen's is clean and creased—apparent evidence of her excellent motivation and desire to succeed. However, as a result of Ellen's learning disability (LD), the writing in her notebook is indecipherable to anyone but Ellen herself. Sometimes even she cannot read what she has written only hours earlier. She knows that her handwriting does not compare favorably with the other girls' cursive, and to make matters worse, Mr. Gunderson's passionate and high-speed lecture style forces her to write as fast as she can.

Nonetheless, this notebook is Ellen's primary study tool. After supper every Thursday, Ellen reads these class notes aloud, and her mother asks her questions about them to prepare for Friday's quiz. The history textbook is written at a reading level well above Ellen's. She struggles to read it, but she remembers little of it afterward. Ellen has been identified as learning disabled and has received special education support for years. Nonetheless, she struggles daily to complete assignments, study for tests, and keep up with her peers.

Ellen is foundering in the class, despite her consistent effort and adults' support. She dreads Friday quizzes, largely because she often cannot read the questions well enough to understand what Mr. Gunderson is asking. If she doesn't pass the state history exam, she will graduate with only a certificate, in lieu of a "real" diploma. Without a "real" diploma, she will be ineligible for admission to public colleges in her state, and since the cost of private colleges far exceeds her family's modest means, Ellen faces the prospect of adulthood without a professional career and the middle-class lifestyle that goes with it.

At 10:00 a.m., Andy walks in and noisily drops his book on top of an unoccupied desk in the last row. Mr. Gunderson scowls, and Andy declares that he is sorry and that it will not happen again. A wave of giggles passes through the room; they have heard that one before. As Mr. Gunderson turns to the chalkboard to continue his lecture, Andy slips a stick of gum into his mouth. He quickly succumbs to boredom and restlessness. In the past, he has found that by making a few off-the-cuff comments, or by asking ridiculous questions, rephrasing them, and asking again, he can force Mr. Gunderson to cease lecturing and focus on him. Andy decides that today he will shout out incorrect answers to Mr. Gunderson's questions, and ask follow-up questions as well, pretending to be sincerely interested in history. As Andy expects, Mr. Gunderson chides him repeatedly for speaking out of turn.

With each of Andy's wisecracks, Mr. Gunderson's anger increases. Try as he might, he cannot conceal this from his students, and soon a wave of grins and giggles follows each of Andy's outbursts. Fortunately, the bell signaling the end of the class period rings, and the class spills out into the hall. Mr. Gunderson shouts to Andy that he wants to speak to him, but Andy ignores him and is gone. With a sigh, Gunderson reaches for his lecture notes for the next period's class. He's not certain how long he can continue in this way. Many of his students are clearly not learning, and he is discouraged. He knows that most of them struggle to read and understand the textbook, and they do not seem to be paying attention when he tries to present the information verbally, accompanied by PowerPoint. His goal, for his students to understand the historical material specified by his state's learning standards, seems far out of the reach of many in his class. They cannot learn from a textbook that they cannot read, and their attention wanders when he lectures. He is at a loss. The only bright spot in Gunderson's professional world is the possibility that he may pick up some helpful tips during the professional development course in Universal Design for Learning (UDL) that he is enrolling in next week. UDL is a blueprint for providing flexible goals, methods, materials, and assessments to meet the learning needs of all students, including those with disabilities (Rose & Meyer, 2002). The four teachers in his building who participated last semester seem to have enjoyed the course.

THE BIG PICTURE

As of 2001, students with specific LD, including dyslexia, ADHD, etc., comprised slightly over 45 percent of all K–12 students with disabilities (National Center for Education Statistics, 2003). While not all of these students struggle to extract meaning from print, they all evidence unique and challenging learning needs of varying degrees of intensity. A large majority of students with LD struggle with print materials, however, and both special education and civil rights laws have repeatedly confirmed the rights of students with disabilities to equal learning opportunities, including access to appropriate and accessible textbooks.

In addition to the longstanding requirements of the Individuals with Disabilities Act (IDEA) and civil rights legislation, the No Child Left Behind Act of 2001 (NCLB) enacted these "equal opportunity" requirements within the context of the Adequate Yearly Progress (AYP) mandates. Established by individual states, AYP is the annual benchmark against which schools are measured. It requires all schools to provide achievement data in reading/language arts, mathematics, and either graduation rate (for high schools and districts) or attendance rate (for elementary and middle/junior high schools). Schools that do not meet the AYP goals in each of these three areas may be identified as "needing improvement." Finally, AYP requires a disaggregation of student achievement data by economic background, race, ethnicity, English proficiency, and disability. The intent of separately assessing the progress of students in these subcategories is to assure an eventual parity in achievement for students perceived as disadvantaged.

The specifics of annual progress monitoring that emphasize the achievement of students with disabilities have moved into the educational spotlight. As states have implemented various forms of large-scale assessment to gather AYP data, it has become increasingly clear that the majority of these assessments have not been designed to address the needs of students with disabilities. States have also discovered that the core curriculum resources available to these students are often ill-suited to meet their learning needs. What is now apparent is that the achievement of students with disabilities must be assessed by the same instruments that chart the progress of general education students and that these instruments must be accessible and flexible enough to measure these students' learning accurately. Concomitantly, the curriculum resources—textbooks—that are intended to enable these students to acquire these skills also need to be appropriate for their use, otherwise these students are denied the opportunity to learn.

The Limits of Print

Much in the same way that students with visual impairments cannot read a standard sixth-grade history textbook because they cannot see it, students with learning and attentional disabilities and those with limited motivation cannot keep pace in the same class—not because they find the history content too challenging—but because they cannot read or attend sufficiently to keep pace with their nondisabled peers. In such circumstances, if these students have access to alternative representations of the printed work (i.e., audio versions via synthetic speech or recorded human voice) they will not be denied access to educational achievement opportunities solely on the basis of their print disability.

The debilitating impact of print disabilities has emerged continually through the data compiled from the National Longitudinal Transition Study-2 (Levine & Wagner, 2004). Of students with LD on individualized education programs (IEP) or Section 504 plans, 41.2% had tests read to them as an accommodation, a percentage higher than for students with visual impairments, at 35.5% (Levine & Wagner, 2003). Similarly, 65% were designated "additional time required to complete assignments" (Levine & Wagner, 2003). Clearly, the reliance on print materials in the process of education has a profound and compromising impact on students with LD.

Increased Expectations

No Child Left Behind has increased expectations and accountability for *all* students, including those with disabilities, to access, participate, and progress in the general curriculum. In order to ensure that every student is able to achieve in the general curriculum, teachers must individualize instruction to the greatest extent possible.

One critical barrier to individualizing instruction is the curriculum itself. Rather than offering multiple gateways to learning and understanding, the "one size fits all" printed textbooks and other resources that make up the general curriculum often serve as barriers (Rose & Meyer, 2002). While conventional materials are reasonably accessible to many students, they clearly present significant barriers for students with sensory or motor disabilities, with low cognitive abilities, and with attentional and organizational problems. They also present more subtle yet equally pervasive barriers for the largest population of identified special education students—those with LD (Pisha, 2003; Pisha & Coyne, 2001).

With fixed, uniform learning materials, teachers are left with the burden of individualizing instruction by providing supplementary adaptations or accommodations. Unfortunately, few teachers have either the time or the expertise to adapt the curriculum materials adequately enough to meet the diverse needs of their students (Ellis & Sabornie, 1990; Moon, Callahan, & Tomlinson, 1999). Moreover, while some teachers are able to adapt materials for accessibility, it is much more difficult to adapt them for instruction. Doing so requires careful attention to ensure that the goals for instruction are preserved in spite of the adaptations, and to ensure that adequate learning progress has been achieved (Edyburn, 2003; Rose & Meyer, 2002). In addition, teachers' efforts are sometimes ineffective because students perceive the adaptations as "different," feel stigmatized by them, and are therefore reluctant to use them (Ellis, 1997).

If students with print-related disabilities are not provided with accessible and appropriate instructional materials at the same time as their nondisabled classmates, the likelihood of their being able to meet standards-based achievement expectations is slim. In the classroom, performance-based accountability pressures, including awareness that the fixed nature of most core instructional materials limits students' opportunity to learn and the increasing accountability expectations of NCLB, all require teachers to seek alternate solutions. The irony of the situation is that while teachers are increasingly provided with well-researched, thoughtfully edited, standards-aligned core instructional materials, that content is "trapped" in the inflexible medium of printed text—and so must be either retrofitted or transformed into more accessible formats for students with disabilities or other learning challenges. This consumes the precious time of teachers, paraprofessionals, special education personnel, or administrators—often detracting from the preparation, planning, and instruction that they should be able to focus on.

Benefits of Universally Designed Instructional Materials

Modern digital materials can present the same content as printed books, but in a format that is much more flexible and accessible. For students who cannot see the words or images, the digital version can be produced in braille or voice, and text-based descriptions of images can be provided. For students who cannot hold the printed book or turn its pages, the virtual pages of a digital book can be turned with slight pressure on a switch. For students who cannot decode the text, any word can be automatically read aloud. For students who lack the background vocabulary of the text, definitions (in English or another language) can be provided with a simple click (Rose & Meyer, 2002).

The advantage of digital formats is that these alternatives, and many others, can be available on an individual basis—available for students who need them, invisible or nondistracting for those who do not. Such customizable alternatives can substantially reduce the barriers found in traditional texts, reducing the effects of what are commonly called "print disabilities."

Digital text is not available for the vast majority of students with disabilities because its benefits are not widely known and simply acquiring these materials can be a challenge. In schools throughout the country, highly motivated teachers invest Herculean efforts in adapting individual books by scanning them into an electronic format to accommodate their students. Some schools and districts are even "digitizing" their entire curriculum. While beneficial for individual students, these local efforts are often costly, redundant, and lacking a research basis (Stahl & Aronica, 2002).

Some states and nonprofit organizations are building more systemic strategies for providing flexible, alternate-format materials, such as audio books and braille texts. While important, these solutions are each designed for students with specific (in most cases, visual) disabilities and are not sufficiently flexible to reach all students.

Nationally, a systematic research-based approach to creating and disseminating digital curriculum materials is emerging. Barriers to developing such an approach include technical, commercial, and legislative factors. The inconsistency of file formats used by publishers and others creating digital materials impedes the creation of flexible digital formats that can be adapted to each individual learner. Educational publishers face challenges in both production and distribution: a conflict between copyright law and federal disability statutes creates problems with permissions and intellectual property. And the novelty of the market for digital materials makes it difficult to create a robust business solution to these challenges.

THE NIMAS INITIATIVE

In the fall of 2002, the U.S. Department of Education created the National File Format Technical Panel to develop a National Instructional Materials Accessibility Standard (NIMAS) for students with disabilities. This panel brought together key stakeholders, including disability advocacy groups, publishers, technology experts, and production and distribution experts.

The goals of this initiative were several. The *overarching goal* was to make appropriate and accessible versions of print textbooks available to every student who needs them. This goal is currently undermined by the inefficiency of the development and distribution system for these materials, which leaves schools struggling to provide instructional materials on a student-by-student basis (particularly for students with print disabilities). Because the system's inefficiency derives in large part from the multiplicity of file formats, the *specific aim* of this work was to make progress toward standardization.

During the course of its three meetings, the Technical Panel built a consensus around the need for a NIMAS to improve access to educational materials for children with disabilities. Consensus was reached on four issues: (a) guiding principles for a NIMAS; (b) baseline format for the NIMAS; (c) application of the format for the NIMAS; and 4) limitations of and restrictions on the NIMAS.

In July 2004 the U.S. Secretary of Education took the precedent-setting step of endorsing the specification recommended by the Panel for NIMAS Version 1.0. This version details the baseline technological specifications for the creation of valid digital source files of preK–12 textbooks and related instructional materials. NIMAS Version 1.0 is sufficiently flexible to create multiple student-ready versions (contracted braille, Digital Talking Book, etc.) from the same publisher-provided source file package, eliminating the need for repetitious and inefficient transformations (print-to-braille, print-to-e-book, etc.). The current standard codifies the minimum requirements for a subset of students with disabilities, particularly those with blindness/low vision and other print disabilities.

NIMAS Mandate in IDEA 2004

In December 2004 NIMAS was included as a mandate for states and publishers in the Individuals with Disabilities Education Improvement Act (IDEA 2004), moving the NIMAS specification from voluntary to required. The NIMAS provisions in IDEA 2004 require state and local education agencies, SEAs and LEAs, to create both a purchasing methodology and a distribution plan for acquiring accessible, alternate-format, student-ready versions of core instructional materials (textbooks) from publishers by December 2006. To facilitate this process, the U.S. Department of Education has established the National Instructional Materials Access Center (NIMAC) as a repository for NIMAS source files provided by publishers. These files will be made available to third-party transformation organizations (Recording for the Blind and Dyslexic, American Printing House for the Blind, etc.) for conversion into student-ready versions. To provide an additional means for states and districts to acquire accessible versions created from NIMAS source files, SEAs and LEAs may also purchase alternate-format versions directly from publishers.

NIMAS marks a major step toward ensuring that the ubiquitous school textbook will be within reach of students with disabilities at the critical point of instruction in an accessible and usable form. NIMAS will, therefore, begin to serve the needs of state and local authorities as they endeavor to provide students with disabilities with the opportunity to learn, a prerequisite for participation in standards-based reform and accountability (Elmore & Fuhrman, 1995; Guiton & Oakes, 1995). Extensions to the standard will be required, however, to address the needs of a wider range of students with disabilities, and a "free market" model that provides high-quality, evidence-based accessible curriculum material while simultaneously compensating the publishers who create them needs to be established.

NIMAS reflects a national consensus of disability advocacy groups, publishers, technology experts, and production and distribution experts. NIMAS details the specifications for the creation of valid digital source files of preK–12 textbooks and related instructional materials. Combined with a package file containing descriptive metadata and PDF files (depicting the layout of the print work), NIMAS files are a flexible foundation for the creation of multiple student-ready versions (braille, Digital Talking Book, etc.)

REMAINING CHALLENGES

The National File Format Technical Panel recognizes that NIMAS will not meet the accessibility needs of all students with disabilities. During the Technical Panel meetings, there was tension between developing a standard that is capable of providing for the accessibility needs of all students with disabilities and the realities of other provisions, such as copyright laws. The publisher members of the Technical Panel expressed concern about adopting a standard that included accessibility features for individuals outside the narrow legal definition of an individual with a print disability, which could potentially encourage violations of the copyright laws. Other members of the panel, however, wanted to ensure that the standard would address the needs of a more comprehensive group of children with disabilities, notwithstanding copyright constraints.

This dilemma affects educators as well, because in spite of the copyright exemption, they have a legal obligation to provide accessible educational materials to all students with disabilities. There is no law that restricts educators from requesting and purchasing accessible versions of educational materials from publishers for use by all students, including students with disabilities. Limited market demand, however, restricts the feasibility of this approach—few publishers have commercially available accessible instructional materials that educators may purchase. Moreover, there is not currently a standard for accessible instructional materials for use by all students with disabilities.

Aware of these issues, the U.S. Department of Education has extended the NIMAS initiative by creating two national centers to continue the NIMAS work. The NIMAS Development Center is working to improve the original standard by identifying new research and technological advances relevant to the standard. This center is also exploring existing and new distribution models for the provision of accessible materials to students with disabilities. The NIMAS Technical Assistance Center works with key stakeholders such as states, school boards, and publishers to raise awareness of the benefits of accessible materials. It also advises stakeholders on the efficient production and distribution of NIMAS-compliant materials.

The NIMAS initiative, while initially focused on a subset of students with disabilities and on the *accessibility* of core instructional materials, lays the foundation for instructional environments that encompass Universal Design for Learning. NIMAS provides incentives for publishers to create and market accessible, alternate-format versions of core instructional materials, and for states to request these materials as assumed options for student use. This "market" approach promises to be free from the existing copyright constraints and means that these additional versions can be made available to any student—those who require them, and those who prefer them as well. The availability of these materials will, in turn, expand the range of instructional opportunities for skilled and committed teachers like Mr. Gunderson, and they will significantly increase the opportunity to learn for students like Eric, Ellen, and Andy.

SPRING IN MR. GUNDERSON'S CLASSROOM

This week, Mr. Gunderson has been teaching lessons that he has created during his participation in a semester-long professional development course in the theory and practice of Universal Design for Learning. He believes that the new view of curriculum and instruction that is a key feature of universal design has the potential both to improve outcomes for all learners in his classroom *and* to help him once again love his job. Even though he has only three computers in his classroom, he is convinced that with smart planning, technology can favorably affect student outcomes. He has designed this new teaching unit with the needs of a wide range of diverse learners in mind, and following the principles of Universal Design for Learning, he has built unprecedented flexibility into his goals, assessments, methods, and materials. This has required considerable thought and hard work, but Mr. Gunderson believes that the results will more than outweigh the cost to him. Even after fifteen years in his profession, he still believes that education is key to success in life and that every child has a right to expect an excellent education.

As today's class files in at 9:45 a.m., they notice that the classroom's arrangement has been changed. Instead of rows facing the chalkboard, desks are arranged in clusters. The classroom's three computers are no longer lined up against the rear wall, but are distributed throughout the room for convenient access and collaborative use.

Today, the class will begin a new unit dealing with the War of 1812. The weekly assignment sheet that Mr. Gunderson hands out differs from those they have received in the past. This raises a quiet buzz of discussion as the class sits down. Most notable on the sheet is the frequent and unprecedented appearance of the words "choose from." The notion of choice of activities and materials is still radical in this environment, and students barely digest this aspect of the plan when they realize that among the choices are listed "work independently or form a group of up to four students for this week's classes." When Andy drifts in five minutes late, even he immediately notices that all is not as usual. One of his friends signals him to join a group seated near one of the computers, and he does so.

Mr. Gunderson begins by briefly explaining that he is experimenting with a new way of approaching teaching and learning, and that he would welcome comments on this new model after class. Several students roll their eyes; they have heard it all before, but most youngsters affect guarded optimism.

The unit begins with an essential question. This question reflects the "big picture" of what Gunderson expects the class to learn this week, and is explicitly linked to the state history standards, which will certainly appear on the high stakes test. This immediately heightens Ellen's attention. She is all about passing that test! Andy scowls, unconvinced, but the other boys in his little cluster do not notice. Their curiosity is aroused, and any change from the same old, same old could only be an improvement. One of them even hazards a response to a question Mr. Gunderson addresses to the class. For several others in the class, beginning the class with a question, rather than a fact or an assertion of the topic's importance, has engaged them and stimulated their curiosity.

Rather than revealing the answer to the essential question, as the class expects, Mr. Gunderson instead directs their attention to the week's plan, and begins to distribute a single photocopied sheet to students containing an account of the War of 1812 culled from *The Diary of Susanna Merritt*, an historical novel about a twelve-year-old girl. Students are asked to study its contents in one of three ways over the next ten minutes: They may read the sheet to themselves and discuss it with another student or the members of their small group; they may listen while a member of their group reads it aloud to the group; or they may access a Web-based copy of the sheet on one of the class computers, with the option of having the text read aloud to them by the computer.

They also notice that their choices for reading an associated textbook chapter and Susanna Merritt's *Diary* are quite different from their usual mandated readings. Most salient to the class is the option of "reading" any or all other assignments in the traditional manner or reading them on a computer. Computers in the classroom, the school library, and in their study halls have been loaded with the required text and a program that can both read the text aloud to them and facilitate their access to the information. These digital versions offer a convenient glossary, ancillary readings containing background knowledge that they may find helpful, and text-to-speech capabilities that can help those who need decoding support to read the text. On request, Mr. Gunderson will provide students with a CD containing both the texts and the supporting software for use on their home computers, or an MP3 audio version of the required reading that can be "read aloud" by any computer or downloaded to a portable MP3 player. Even Andy suspects that this may be an interesting week.

As the class files out, Ellen finds herself with Eric, as both of them have chosen to ask Mr. Gunderson for a copy of "that CD," for use on home computers. They studiously ignore each other, for different reasons, and neither plans to announce to their friends that they "got the CD." Nonetheless, each does take a copy home and installs it immediately after supper.

That evening, Ellen finishes reading her history assignment in thirty minutes; her home computer pronounced the words that Ellen could not decode independently. The role of her mother has shifted from that of a reader to that of a co-discussant. They focus on the ideas in the passages, not on the struggle to read the words. Mrs. Jones is flabbergasted. She has read her daughter's textbooks to her for several years and has worried that her daughter's LD would seriously limit her prospects as an adult. As she prepares for bed, she shares her observations with her husband.

Eric also uses the CD that evening. While its range of options for text access and additional background information are initially distracting, his natural inquisitiveness propels him to discover a new way to increase his attention to the task. By setting the software's sequential text highlighting feature to "read" sentence-by-sentence in conjunction with the computer's high-quality synthetic speech, he discovers that he is able to maintain his focus. His eyes seem drawn to the highlighted words. He also discovers that he is able to use the computer's "find" function to help him answer the questions that appear at the end of the chapter in a way that he was never able to accomplish with the print version.

Although Andy was unwilling to voice his interest in class, he chooses to work with the *Diary of Susanna Merritt*. He is interested to discover that the book, though fictional, is faithful to the historical events described in the textbook. Furthermore, even though the heroine is a girl, the fact that she was the same age meant that she was dealing with some of the same issues he is. He likes approaching the subject matter through the eyes of a "person," and feels he can relate to her interactions with friends and family during a time of war.

On Tuesday Mr. Gunderson informs the class that from this point forward, all readings assigned from the class textbook will also be available on CD for home use, as well as on computers around the school. He had received three telephone calls from parents who wanted to know more about the "changes in history class" the night before, and each parent expressed support for the changes he had instituted. Mr. Gunderson usually dreaded evening parent calls; invariably, the callers were upset or even angry. Three supportive calls from parents in a single evening was unprecedented.

MOVING THE PROMISE FORWARD

For the first time in the history of federal special education legislation, the government is addressing the appropriateness of core instructional textbooks to meet the needs of students with disabilities. As the result of unprecedented agreement among disability advocates, curriculum publishers, and educators, the immediate and distinct needs of students who evidence a "print disability" as the result of a sensory or physical impairment will be met. This initiative creates the foundation for expanding these alternatives to every other student with a disability, and for those students who might simply prefer to work with more flexible and supportive materials. This expansion of opportunity will help teachers like Mr. Gunderson to align the richness of his curriculum to both the learning needs of his students and the achievement requirements of his school district and state. For Ellen, Andy, and Eric, it promises to increase their inclusion in general education, heighten their engagement with learning, and, ultimately, raise their academic achievement beyond the limits of their disabilities.

REFERENCES

Edyburn, D. L. (2003). Measuring assistive technology outcomes in reading. *Journal of Special Education Technology, 18*(1). Retrieved May 18, 2005, from http://jset.unlv.edu/18.1/asseds/edyburn.html

Ellis, E. (1997). Watering up the curriculum for adolescents with learning disabilities: Goals of the knowledge dimension. *Remedial and Special Education, 18*, 326–346.

Ellis, E. S., & Sabornie, E. J. (1990). Strategy-based adaptive instruction in content-area classes: Social validity of six options. *Teacher Education and Special Education, 13*, 133–144.

Elmore, R. F., & Fuhrman, S. H. (1995). Opportunity-to-learn standards and the state role in education. *Teachers College Record, 96*, 433–458.

Guiton, G., & Oakes, J. (1995). Opportunity to learn and conceptions of educational equality. *Educational Evaluation and Policy Analysis, 17*, 323–336.

Levine, P., & Wagner, M. (2004). *Secondary school students' experiences in secondary education classrooms* (National Longitudinal Transition Study-2). Menlo Park, CA: SRI.

Moon, T. R., Callahan, C. M., & Tomlinson, C. A. (1999). The effects of mentoring relationships on preservice teachers' attitudes toward academically diverse students. *Gifted Child Quarterly, 43*(2), 56–62.

National Center for Education Statistics. (2003). Table 52. Children 3 to 21 years old served in federally supported programs for the disabled, by type of disability: Selected years, 1976–77 to 2001–02. In *Digest of education statistics tables and figures, 2003.* Washington, DC: U.S. Department of Education. Retrieved May 5, 2005, from http://nces.ed.gov/programs/digest/d03/tables/dt052.asp

Pisha, B. (2003). Assistive technologies: making a difference. *IDA Perspectives, 29*(4), 1, 4.

Pisha, B., & Coyne, P. (2001). Smart from the start: The promise of universal design for learning. *Remedial and Special Education, 22,* 197–203.

Rose, D. H., & Meyer, A. (2002). *Teaching every student in the digital age: Universal design for learning.* Alexandria, VA: ASCD.

Stahl, S., & Aronica, M. (2002). Digital text in the classroom. *Journal of Special Education Technology, 17*(2). Retrieved May 18, 2005, from http://jset.unlv.edu/17.2/asseds/rose.html

CHAPTER NINE

Transforming the Textbook to Improve Learning

SKIP STAHL

INTRODUCTION

Today's classrooms house an increasingly diverse student population, including not only students with widely different social, economic, cultural, and language backgrounds, but also students with a wide range of physical, cognitive, and sensory disabilities. The federal No Child Left Behind Act (NCLB) of 2001 and the Individuals with Disabilities Education Act (IDEA) of 1997 mandate increased expectations and accountability for this diverse range of students to access, participate, and progress in the general curriculum. In order to ensure that all of these students are able to achieve in the general curriculum, particularly in light of such disparate strengths and needs, teachers must individualize instruction.

One critical barrier to individualizing instruction is the curriculum itself. Rather than offering multiple gateways to learning and understanding, the "one size fits all" printed textbooks and other resources that make up the general curriculum often serve as barriers. While conventional materials are reasonably accessible to many students, they clearly present significant barriers for students with sensory or motor disabilities. They also present a challenge to students with low cognitive abilities and those with attentional and organizational problems, and more subtle, yet equally pervasive, barriers for the largest population of identified special education students—those with learning disabilities.

With fixed, uniform learning materials, teachers are left with the burden of individualizing instruction by providing supplementary adaptations or accommodations. Unfortunately, few teachers have either the time or expertise to adapt the curriculum materials adequately to meet the diverse needs of their students (Ellis & Sabornie, 1990; Moon, Callahan, & Tomlinson, 1999). Moreover, while some teachers are able to adapt materials for accessibility, it is a different matter to adapt them for instruction. Doing so requires careful attention to ensure that the goals for instruction are preserved in spite of the adaptations and to ensure that adequate learning progress has been achieved (Rose & Meyer, 2002; Edyburn, 2004). Furthermore, teachers' efforts sometimes are ineffective because students perceive the adaptations as "different," feel stigmatized by them, and are therefore reluctant to use them (Ellis, 1997).

SCOPE OF THE CHALLENGE

In the majority of the nation's approximately 100,000 public and private K–12 schools, textbooks are the primary curriculum material. Eighty to ninety percent of grade 4–12 math and science classrooms use textbooks (Hudson, McMahon, & Overstreet, 2002), and that figure is similar for reading and language arts instruction (NCREL, 2000). The average yearly expenditure for textbooks and related materials in each of these 100,000 schools is approximately $10,000 per school per year (Peter Li Education Group, 2002). In addition to the fact that textbooks are the principal learning resource for general education students, their use by students with disabilities increases steadily as these students progress through the educational system. As reported from the National Longitudinal Transition Study-2 (NLTS2):

> Students with learning disabilities, emotional disturbances, or speech, sensory, or other health impairments are among the most likely to use textbooks often (61% to 72% do so, compared with 41% of students with autism, p < .001 for most comparisons), at least in part because they also are the most likely to have experiences reported for academic subject classes. (Levine & Wagner, 2004)

If the achievement of students with disabilities is to be assessed by the same instruments that chart the progress of general education students, these instruments need to be accessible and flexible enough to chart these students' skills accurately. Concomitantly, the curriculum resources—textbooks—that these students are provided with to acquire these skills also need to be accessible and appropriate from the outset.

ACCOUNTABILITY RAISES THE BAR

The preface to Section 1 of No Child Left Behind succinctly frames the purpose of the legislation: "To close the achievement gap with accountability, flexibility, and choice, so that no child is left behind." In the four years since its enactment, the majority of teachers, school administrators, and school boards have focused on its accountability mandates, while parents and advocates have attended to its provisions for choice, especially in terms of school placement. Surprisingly, NCLB's third key component, flexibility, received significantly less attention in the months immediately following the bill's passage. In many cases, it wasn't until the annual reporting mechanisms of the legislation's Adequate Yearly Progress (AYP) requirements were implemented that the issue of flexibility increased in importance.

Adequate Yearly Progress is the annual benchmark against which schools are measured. All schools must provide achievement data in four separate areas: reading/language arts, mathematics, and either graduation rate (for high schools and districts) or attendance rate (for elementary and middle/junior high schools). Schools that do not meet annual progress goals (as established by individual states) in each of these three areas may be identified as "needing improvement." Finally, AYP is also dependent upon a disaggregation of student achievement data by economic background, race, ethnicity, English proficiency, and disability. The intent of separately assessing the progress of students in these subcategories is to assure an eventual parity in achievement for students perceived as disadvantaged—the "achievement gap" students.

The combination of annual progress monitoring with a deliberate emphasis on students with disabilities quickly caught the attention of school, district, and state education personnel. Between 2001 and 2004 most states had moved toward some form of large-scale assessment in order to gather the achievement data that the AYP process required; very few of these assessment initiatives adequately addressed the needs of students with disabilities, despite the fact that NCLB was specific in its intent that the majority of enrolled students were expected to participate. Furthermore, NCLB clearly required these large-scale assessments to "be designed to be valid and accessible for use by the widest possible range of students, including students with disabilities and students with limited English proficiency." Many educators presumed that the majority of students with disabilities would qualify for "alternate" assessments. This perception led to a qualification from the U.S. Department of Education in December of 2003. The Department said that NCLB limits participation in alternate assessment to 1 percent of the total student population (approximately 9 percent of identified special education students), and that the majority of special education students were expected to participate in the same assessments as their nondisabled peers.

In contrast to previous statutes (PL94-142; IDEA; Section 504; ADA), which mandated either unique services or equal access, but left compliance to be shaped by the complaints or litigation of the very individuals these laws sought to protect, accountability under NCLB was designed to reflect the responsiveness and quality of the educational system itself. As a consequence, classrooms, schools, districts, and states must pay as much attention to the achievement of students identified as "disadvantaged" (including those with disabilities) as they pay to any other students.

Not surprisingly, the accountability mandates of NCLB have increased consideration of large-scale assessments that are designed from the beginning to be accessible to students with disabilities (Thompson & Thurlow, 2002; Dolan & Hall, 2001, 2003; Abell, Bauder, & Simmons, 2004). These investigations have in turn prompted a reanalysis of classroom practices (Bowe, 1999; Orkwis, 2003), the achievement standards on which they are based (McDonnell, McLaughlin, & Morison, 1997; Gloeckler, 2001; Thurlow, 2002), and with intense scrutiny, the textbooks that create the foundation for instructional materials in the majority of the nation's schools (Orkwis, 1999; Gordon, 2002; Perl & Gordon, 2003; Dalton, 2003).

EXISTING SOLUTIONS: THE MATERIALS

Alternate-format materials are commonly provided to students with disabilities in one of four categories: braille, audio, large print, and e-text. An overview of how materials in each of these four categories are created, made available to, and used by students is presented below.

Braille

For more than 100 years the American Printing House for the Blind (APH) has created books in alternate accessible formats, including braille, supported by an annual federal appropriation. In the early 1900s, Congress began requiring that copies of embossed books be provided to the Library of Congress, and in the 1930s, concurrent with the establishment of a uniform system of braille, Congress established the National Library Service for the Blind and Physically Handicapped (NLS) at the Library of Congress. One of the purposes of establishing NLS was to provide federal coordination of the process of braille production and distribution. In addition to these large national braille production and distribution centers, additional regional and state braille distribution systems have been developed in an effort to keep braille editions current and readily available. A number of private braille production companies have also been established to augment government-supported efforts.

For much of the past century, the process of creating braille has been one of retrofitting existing print works into embossed versions. Of necessity, this has involved obtaining, storing, and transcribing the print versions, re-creating the work in an embossed format, validating and proofing the embossed version, and mailing these versions to the braille readers who have requested them. In addition to the complexity and time required to complete this process, the ratio of embossed braille pages to pages of print is approximately 6 to 1: a 500-page print book would require nearly 3,000 pages of embossed braille.

During the past three decades, refreshable braille displays (RBDs) have evolved to create temporary print-to-braille transformations. RBDs receive digital information—braille-formatted ASCII text, for example—and transform it into braille characters that are then displayed on a flexible membrane via a series of movable pins. RBDs offer considerable improvement over embossed braille in their portability and ability to create "braille on the fly," but their high cost limits their widespread use.

Regardless of limitations, RBDs highlight the incredible potential of digital media to revolutionize the braille creation process. As more curriculum publishers adopt a digital workflow—creating digital source files at the beginning of the production process rather than at its end—the potential of creating braille-ready digital versions without having to retrofit existing print works becomes technologically feasible. This possibility, with its attendant elimination of the inefficiencies and inaccuracies associated with the creation of braille as an afterthought in the book production process, provides the foundation for the National Instructional Materials Accessibility Standard (NIMAS) detailed below.

Audio

In the early 1930s, the American Foundation for the Blind (AFB) and its collaborating research partners pioneered the "Talking Book." Originally created on acetate and vinyl records, this new audio format provided print-disabled users with recorded human narration and some rudimentary navigation, and it quickly became popular. The new format steadily evolved into four-track cassettes and, for the past thirty years, has been the primary format of both NLS and Recording for the Blind and Dyslexic.

Concurrent with the development of digital source files as the preferred medium for the efficient creation of braille, digital versions of audio books have also evolved. Research and development during the past fifteen years led to the approval of the "Digital Talking Book" standard by National Information Standards Organization (NISO) and the American National Standards Institute (ANSI) as ANSI/NISO Z39.86-2002. Synonymous with "DAISY 3," a "Digital Audio-based Information System" format developed by the international DAISY Consortium, this ANSI/NISO standard provided the foundation elements of the recently endorsed National Instructional Materials Accessibility Standard (NIMAS). Regardless of which "flavor" of the standard is applied, Digital Talking Books hold enormous potential. This format supports recorded human audio either as a stand-alone medium or synchronized to onscreen text, extensive navigation, support for additional media (images, charts and graphs, even video), and, by design, well-formatted braille.

While these broad-based initiatives have been evolving at the national and international levels, special educators, assistive technology vendors, and students have also capitalized on readily available and cost effective digital solutions. The use of text in electronic formats (e-text) by students with disabilities has increased exponentially in the past ten years, and students with visual, learning, and attentional disabilities have experienced enormous benefits from the flexibility these formats have offered. Students with visual impairments may use screen readers such as JAWS or WindowEyes to have any onscreen text spoken aloud, while students who do not need to have the entire computer interface read aloud may use supported readers like WYNN, Kurzweil, Read&Write, ReadPlease, and eReader to have text spoken aloud by synthetic speech. The majority of these assistive technologies will auditorize files created in Microsoft Word, RTF, ASCII, or HTML, yielding a high degree of flexibility. Many of these software applications are now being expanded to accommodate the emerging Digital Talking Book (DAISY) format as well.

Large Print

Many of the libraries and production houses that produce or distribute braille and Talking Books also produce large-print books. The National Library Service maintains a list of large-print production and distribution facilities in the United States. The use of large-print materials, while fairly common among older adults with vision loss, is less common in schools. The American Printing House for the Blind does produce large-print textbooks, and a number of commercial publishers routinely produce large-print versions for sale, although the use of these materials in the nation's classrooms is limited.

E-Text

In today's classrooms, the e-text is a primary alternate format. With the exception of braille, e-text formats such as Word, RTF, ASCII, and HTML can provide each of the accommodations that are singly offered by audio-only and large print. E-text can be highlighted (selected with a mouse or key combination) and read aloud by synthetic speech on almost any computer. While the tonal quality of computer-generated speech is not as good as a recorded human voice, it is far more flexible; continuing research in this area has resulted in increasingly high-quality pronunciation. E-text can be instantly increased in size, preferential color schemes can be applied, and letters, words, phrases, sentence, paragraphs, and sections can be sequentially highlighted as the text is read aloud.

In the past ten years, the cost of desktop computer technology has steadily decreased, while its capabilities have steadily increased. Ten years ago, digital scanning equipment and software, required to transform print into digital text, cost thousands; today it costs hundreds. Once a rarity, this technology is now common in schools and provides educators with the ability to themselves transform inaccessible print works into accessible digital formats. Faced with the mandates of federal special education and civil rights laws, special educators have turned to this solution.

While this approach to providing accessible versions of print curriculum materials is pragmatic and effective, it also diverts the available educational resources to product retrofitting and file format production— neither of which is an efficient use of instructional resources. These local solutions also result in materials of varying quality and usability, and often end up meeting only the needs of an individual student, with no potential for broader use. Clearly, the acknowledged efficiencies offered by digital tools and formats need to be combined with a national agenda in order to eliminate redundancies and allow educators to return to the task of instruction.

COPYRIGHT LAW AND EFFORTS TO INCREASE WIDESPREAD AVAILABILITY

As part of the 1966 revisions to the Copyright Act, Section 121—known as the "Chafee Amendment"—was enacted to allow alternate-format creation by "a nonprofit organization or governmental agency that has a primary mission to provide specialized services relating to training, education, or adaptive reading or information access needs of blind or disabilities, particularly those with blindness/low vision and other print disabilities.

On December 3, 2004, President Bush signed the Individuals with Disabilities Education Improvement Act of 2004 into law. This reauthorization built upon the secretary of education's endorsement of NIMAS by codifying the specification into mandates for state and local education agencies. In addition, Congress authorized the secretary of education to establish a National Instructional Materials Access Center (NIMAC) to provide a central point of distribution for NIMAS files. In Part B of IDEA 2004 in Sections 612 (State Eligibility) and 613 (Local Education Agency Eligibility), state and local education authorities (SEAs and LEAs) are now required to establish procedures with curriculum publishers for ensuring that NIMAS-conforming digital source files are provided to NIMAC for subsequent transformation into accessible formats—braille, Digital Talking Book, large print, etc. Alternatively, SEAs and LEAs can meet the NIMAS mandate by documenting that they have entered into a contractual relationship with curriculum publishers to purchase these specialized formats directly. In either case, the intent of both the NIMAS and the NIMAC mandates is to assure that students with print disabilities are provided with accessible and appropriate alternative versions of print instructional materials at the same time that the print versions are made available to other students.

NIMAS marks a major step toward ensuring that the ubiquitous textbook will be within reach of students with disabilities at the critical point of instruction in an accessible and usable form. NIMAS will therefore begin to serve the needs of state and local authorities as they endeavor to provide students with disabilities with the opportunity to learn, a prerequisite for participation in standards-based reform and accountability (Elmore & Fuhrman, 1995; Guiton & Oakes, 1995). NIMAS 1.0 is an essential first step that provides the foundation for the subsequent creation of a variety of alternate-format versions designed to meet the needs of students with a range of disabilities.

To extend this initiative, the Department of Education has recently awarded two cooperative agreements to CAST to continue the NIMAS initiative. The NIMAS Development Center will continue the refinement

other persons with disabilities," without seeking permission from the copyright holder. The purpose of the Chafee Amendment was to institutionalize a process by which these specialized organizations could provide alternate-format materials and to clarify the ambiguities inherent in existing "Fair Use" requirements. The Chafee exemption was designed to expedite the creation and availability of accessible versions of selected print works ("non-dramatic literary works") in "specialized" formats to "qualified" individuals.

While this exemption has significantly facilitated the capacity of educational institutions, both K–12 and postsecondary, to meet the needs of students with disabilities, its requirements have also emerged as ambiguous. As a consequence, many education personnel who provide services to students with disabilities have come to assume that any "special" educator or disability support specialist may obtain or create an accessible version in any format for any disabled student struggling with access to print. Discrepancies in the interpretation of Chafee constraints are not limited to educators, however, since even widely acknowledged "authorized entities" such as Recording for the Blind and Dyslexic and the National Library Service for the Blind apply differing interpretations.

Regardless of whether the Chafee exemption is interpreted narrowly or broadly, its enactment set a precedent in its affirmation of the right of "print-disabled" individuals to be provided timely access to the same information as is available to their nondisabled peers, and pursuant to Section 504 of the Rehabilitation Act, that access should be provided in the format most appropriate to their needs. The fact that some students with learning disabilities may not qualify under existing Chafee guidelines, or that students with attentional, cognitive, or hearing disabilities are, in fact, excluded, collides with the "Access, Participation and Progress" requirements of IDEA and the "Equal Access" requirements of the Rehabilitation Act and the ADA. It is precisely this collision that has motivated educators and disability service providers to err on the side of civil rights legislation and federal special education law when determining which students receive accessible materials and when.

In the long run, the current Chafee exemption provides an inadequate foundation for the large-scale provision of alternate-format materials for students with print disabilities, simply because it was designed to meet the needs of a small subset of individuals on a case-by-case basis. In order to address the ever-increasing national demand for accessible instructional materials while simultaneously maintaining compliance with intellectual property law, new enterprise-level solutions need to be created.

Thirty-one states now have alternate-format requirements specifically relating to the provision of files for the creation of braille versions of print textbooks (AFB, 2003). In addition, a smaller but expanding number of states (Arizona, California, Georgia, Kentucky, New Mexico, and New York) either require publishers to provide accessible versions of textbooks, require publishers to provide digital versions, or give preference to publishers who provide accessible versions (Perl & Gordon, 2003).

While the braille laws are longstanding, the expanded state legislation requiring accessible or digital versions of textbooks for a broader category of "print-disabled" students has been enacted in the past seven years, primarily as the result of that Section 121 copyright exemption, the Chafee Amendment.

The Chafee Amendment enlisted "authorized entities" to provide "blind or other persons with disabilities" with accessible versions of print materials in "specialized formats." Originally intended as a means of providing print-disabled individuals with accessible versions, Chafee has come to be used by special education personnel in schools and content transformation organizations (Recording for the Blind and Dyslexic, BookShare, etc.) as the basis for the large-scale creation and distribution of accessible textbooks, without compensation to either publishers or rights holders. This widespread application of Chafee has generated considerable concern among publishers and copyright holders (Adler, 2002), some of whom believe that many current initiatives exceed the Chafee restrictions.

The current system of creating and distributing alternate-format instructional materials to print-disabled students is a patchwork of national and local efforts. Conversion entities and repositories who perceive themselves to be "Chafee-compliant" offer a range of alternate formats.

Recording for the Blind and Dyslexic produces audio versions, Share produces digital text versions in the Digital Talking Book fo American Printing House for the Blind produces both embossec electronic braille and large print, American Foundation for the produces Digital Talking Books, the National Library Service fo Blind produces Digital Talking Books and braille. For-profit com cial entities such as Duxbury Braille Systems, ghBraille, and others contribute their expertise to the other providers or directly to states districts. Finally, with the advent of cost-effective and efficient di scanning technology, local districts and schools have significantly creased their capacities to digitize books directly into more access digital formats.

While this array of efforts reflects both the importance of altern format materials and the deep commitment of alternate-format prov ers, it is also rife with redundancy, inefficiency, and inaccuracy. The c rent options for acquiring alternate formats also result in the creation materials that vary widely in quality, and perpetuate a process of loc ized and highly "disability-specific" solutions in which efforts to supp one subgroup of students with disabilities often do little to support t needs of the other groups.

WORKING TOWARD A NATIONAL APPROACH

On July 27, 2004, the United States Department of Education official ly endorsed the National Instructional Materials Accessibility Standarc (NIMAS). This voluntary file format reflects the consensus of disabilit advocacy groups, publishers, technology experts, and production anc distribution experts. Version 1.0 of NIMAS details the baseline techno logical specifications for the creation of valid digital source files of preK– 12 textbooks and related instructional materials. NIMAS Version 1.0 is sufficiently flexible to create multiple student-ready versions (contracted braille, Digital Talking Book, etc.) from the same publisher-provided source file package, eliminating the need for repetitious and inefficient transformations (print-to-braille, print-to-ebook, etc.). The current standard codifies the minimum requirements for a subset of students with

of the NIMAS standard, and the NIMAS Technical Assistance Center will provide support to states, publishers, and other stakeholders in implementing the standard nationwide.

BENEFITS OF ACCESSIBLE TEXTBOOKS

What instructional realities underlie the exponential increase in the national, state, and local attention that is being paid to accessible instructional materials, and how will the increased availability and quality of these materials increase student achievement?

For Students with Visual Impairments

Approximately 94,000 blind/low-vision students are provided special education support under IDEA; for the vast majority of these students, access to alternate-format materials is essential (American Foundation for the Blind, 2003). For a subset of this population, braille versions of textbooks are the preferred format. On a daily basis in every state, the timely provision of quality braille textbooks depends upon the seamless cooperation of a dispersed network of publishers, textbook adoption entities, alternate-format providers, braille transcribers, teachers of the visually impaired, and students. Even when this network of support and provision works efficiently, the time and money required to produce braille is staggering. As McCarthy (2002) told the U.S. Senate:

> A book the size of the biology text I have with me today will take approximately nine months to transcribe. Most transcribers work on several books at one time—and regularly provide volumes of braille to stay ahead of the class syllabus. A book like this—1,183 pages—would translate into 4,732 pages in braille. The average cost to produce this braille book would be $16,562.

Thirty-one states with "braille laws" require textbook publishers to provide digital files compatible for braille transcription. These required formats include ASCII, ICADD-22, SGML, BRF, Word, and RTF. In addition, the majority of states require these files to be provided free of charge. As a consequence, publishers must generate multiple files in multiple formats for multiple jurisdictions, with no financial incentive to produce anything beyond the baseline requirements. A unified national approach would eliminate many of the current file format incongruities, while simultaneously meeting the requirements of individual states. It would increase the quality of braille-compliant digital files and significantly accelerate the delivery of alternate-format materials to students with visual impairments.

For Students with Physical Disabilities

Approximately 0.8 percent of the population of students receiving services under IDEA and Section 504 of the Rehabilitation Act of 1973, or 188,000 K–12 students, are identified with orthopedic or physical disabilities. While not all of these students experience challenges with print materials, a significant number of them do. The provision of alternate-format materials to students with physical disabilities, while not as multilayered nor as time-consuming as the provision of alternate formats to students with visual impairments, is nevertheless fraught with complexities. Perhaps more important, the digital files that are provided to many states for conversion into braille are generally unsuitable for students whose primary print disability is physical. Since the required digital files are designed primarily to be transformed into a specific "student-ready" format (in most cases, braille) they are not developed with direct display or direct use by students with limited dexterity in mind. It is possible to apply layout and navigation structure (unit, chapter, section, head, subhead, paragraph, etc.) or emphasis (bold for glossary terms, for example) as well as to validate page number correspondence, but this is a time-consuming process and it is often easier and less costly to scan the print version into a digital format. For the majority of students with physical disabilities, navigation through the text becomes a significant issue, since students unable to manage a print book physically are generally unable to use a mouse.

Once supplied with usable structure, the digital file becomes inherently more navigable using voice control, eye gaze, head pointer, single-switch access, or keyboard. Unfortunately, the majority of alternate-format materials created for students with physical disabilities do not contain images or graphics, so these students are often forced to alternate between the on-screen display of text and the graphical elements in the textbook. A more unified approach will allow for the creation of varied, well-structured, and complete student-ready versions. These will include easily navigable digital files with images from the same source file, eliminating redundancies and simultaneously improving the accuracy of the alternate version and aligning it with the print work.

For Students with Learning Disabilities

As of 2001, students with specific learning disabilities (such as dyslexia, ADHD, etc.) comprised slightly over 45 percent of all K–12 students with disabilities (NCES, 2002). While not all of these students struggle to extract meaning from print, and while not all of them may qualify for alternate-format materials under the Section 121 copyright exemption, they all evidence unique and challenging learning needs of varying degrees of intensity. A large majority of learning disabled students do struggle with print materials, however, and setting aside for the moment the issue of who does or who does not qualify for alternate-format materials under existing copyright law, both special education legislation (IDEA) and civil rights laws (ADA, Section 504) have repeatedly reinforced the rights of students with disabilities to equal learning opportunities, including access to appropriate and accessible textbooks.

Much in the same way that students with visual impairments cannot read a standard seventh-grade social studies textbook because they cannot see it, students with learning disabilities cannot keep pace in the same class—not because they find the social studies content too challenging, but because they cannot read sufficiently to keep pace with their nondisabled peers. In these circumstances, if these students have access to alternative representations of the printed work (audio versions, for example, via synthetic speech or recorded human voice), they will then not be denied access to learning opportunities like studying social studies solely on the basis of their print disability.

The debilitating impact of print disabilities continually emerged through the data compiled from the National Longitudinal Transition Study-2 (NLTS2). Of learning-disabled students on IEPs or Section 504 plans, 41.2 percent had tests read to them as an accommodation, a percentage higher than for students with visual impairments

(35.5%) (Levine & Wagner, 2004). Similarly, the percentage who qualified for "additional time required to complete assignments" (65%) was the highest of any population of special education or Section 504 students, with the exception of those with traumatic brain injury (Levine & Wagner, 2004). Clearly the reliance on print materials in education has a profound and compromising impact on learning-disabled students. The availability of textbooks in accessible alternative formats suitable for representation via human or synthetic speech would significantly increase the independent use of these core curriculum resources by students with learning disabilities.

For Students Who Are Deaf or Hard of Hearing

Students with hearing impairments are not routinely considered "print disabled." However, young children with hearing impairments either have little or no exposure to the prosody, vocabulary, syntax, and semantics of spoken language, and it is this foundation upon which the literacy skills of reading and writing are based.

Hearing-impaired students who acquire sign language as their primary medium of communication internalize a linguistic structure that is markedly different from standard English; as a consequence, few deaf students develop beyond a fifth-grade reading level, and this factor alone becomes a significant limitation as these students attempt to progress through school. In fact, some of the most recent research on the literacy level of 17- and 18-year-old deaf students yielded a median reading grade level score of 4.0 on the Stanford 9 (Holt, Traxler, & Allen, 1997).

During the past decade, research has emerged that documents a strong causal relationship between proficiency in sign language (specifically, ASL) and proficiency in standard English (Strong & Prinz, 1997; Prinz & Strong, 1998; Padden & Ramsey, 2000). Researchers who have found promise in this "bilingual" approach to improving deaf literacy also note that providing signed equivalents to standard English (or English equivalents for sign) has generally relied upon the sequential display of information—first sign, then English, for example—primarily because the logistics of creating an accurate, efficient, and practical approach to creating a simultaneous display—both sign and English available at the same time—have been daunting. There is widespread agreement, however, that technologies such as the Signing Avatar and the use of concatenated video recordings of human interpreters can increasingly be combined with the ever-increasing power of computers to create instantaneous onscreen translations from one language to another. The increased availability of digitally based standard textbooks provides the necessary foundation elements for the subsequent creation of learning resources that contain both signed and text versions of the same instructional content.

For Students with Mental Retardation, Traumatic Brain Injury, and Other Cognitive Impairments

This subset of students with IEPs or Section 504 plans, though ineligible for alternate-format materials under the Chafee copyright exemption, often find their educational opportunities limited by the inflexibility of instructional materials. In contrast to the drill and practice approach to basic "sight word" development that permeated the reading instruction of students with cognitive disabilities for many years, recent findings (Gurry & Larkin, 1999; National Reading Panel, 2000) indicate a shift in awareness toward a research-based approach. Koppenhaver, Erickson, and Skotko (2001) and their colleagues at the Center for Literacy and Disability Studies suggest that students with mental retardation benefit from the same research-based instructional approaches that work for other students who are learning to read (National Reading Panel, 2000)—that is, reading instruction that

- focuses on reading for meaning
- provides direct instruction in reading skills such as decoding
- offers appealing print and electronic texts

The type of reading instruction envisioned by the National Reading Panel contributors and by other researchers is readily facilitated by the availability of flexible, adjustable versions of core instructional materials.

Media that can be transformed from one modality to another (text-to-speech, for example) or used to customize the display of a page into discrete and manageable chunks can help to focus the attention of distractible students or help differentiate salient from less-important information. Students with mental retardation often experience difficulty with motivation and attention (Hickson, Blackman, & Reis, 1995). These students clearly benefit from engaging and adjustable displays, or displays that support constrained presentations of information. Furthermore, research has shown that students with mental retardation have difficulty understanding abstract concepts, especially when the abstractions cannot be effectively concretized or represented as an aid to understanding (Beirne-Smith, Ittenbach, & Patton, 1998). Accessible, flexible alternate versions of core curriculum materials can increase engagement, attention, and achievement by offering adjustable levels of complexity, novelty, and mixed media.

CONTINUING CHALLENGES

Technological Challenges

The initiative to establish Version 1.0 of NIMAS is designed to provide the foundation for the subsequent creation of a variety of alternate-format versions designed to meet the needs of students with visual, physical, hearing, learning, and cognitive disabilities. The NIMAS file package will consist of an XML (eXtensible Markup Language) source file and associated PDF (Portable Document Format) files that contain the graphic elements included in print textbooks. One proposed workflow involves the distribution of the NIMAS file package to a centralized repository for validation and subsequent distribution to third-party content conversion organizations (Recording for the Blind and Dyslexic, BookShare, American Printing House for the Blind, etc.), who will in turn create a variety of student-ready versions for distribution to schools and states. Alternatively, the NIMAS file package might be distributed directly to states that have established digitally based alternate-format distribution mechanisms (e.g., Texas Braille Production Center, the Kentucky Digital Text Network, etc.). Regardless of the distribution system established, a number of technological challenges need to be addressed.

Legislative Challenges

Although six states have extended the scope of their existing braille laws to encompass broader requirements for accessible textbooks, problems remain. While these state-level mandates are progressive in their intent and designed to facilitate the state's capacity to meet its obligations under existing federal special education and civil rights laws, they are also duplicative, and in some cases, divisive. Only three of the six states (Kentucky, Arizona, and New Mexico) specifically reference an alignment with a "national file format" (NIMAS) once endorsed by the United States Department of Education; without this acknowledged alignment with a unified national format, some existing and emerging state legislation threatens to perpetuate redundancies and inefficiencies.

In order to prevent this effect, curriculum publishers, third-party content transformation organizations, and disability advocacy groups have proposed and supported first the Instructional Materials Accessibility Act of 2002 (IMAA) and, more recently, the inclusion of mandated NIMAS compliance in the reauthorization of IDEA. Both of these federal legislative efforts are designed to achieve the same goal: a federal mandate for both states and publishers to adopt a unified approach to address this issue.

Commercial Challenges

The systematic provision of accessible alternate-format versions of print materials began with the invention of braille in the early 1800s (Roblin, 1952/1993). The institutionalization of this effort in the United States occurred in the early 1930s with the establishment of the National Library Service for the Blind at the Library of Congress (Perl, 2002). Government-supported organizations like Recording for the Blind and Dyslexic and American Printing House for the Blind were created to address an expanding and differentiated need. The steady emergence of additional nonprofit and for-profit alternate-format organizations during the past fifty years has attested to the sustained need for these materials.

Inherent in these initiatives has been an acknowledgment that the provision of alternate-format versions of print materials is an expensive and time-consuming process. Historically, individuals with "print disabilities" have been provided with these versions at reduced or no charge, and print publishers were expected not to produce this content, but to facilitate its production at little or no cost to the consumer. Since the passage of the first Elementary and Secondary Education Act (ESEA) in 1965, and the subsequent evolution of state departments of education as distribution points for "categorical" aid (Ravitch, 2000), these state-level requirements have steadily increased.

Concurrent with this increased systemic demand, the local (site-based) transformation of print textbooks into accessible digital versions—MS Word or HTML or RTF files, for example—has also increased exponentially. Special education personnel at the state, local, and district levels interpret the Chafee copyright exemption as providing them with a legal means of creating accessible versions of textbooks to students identified as print disabled. While this approach offers a pragmatic solution to meeting the needs of students in a timely manner, very few local efforts include any embedded security (digital rights management) to ensure their limited distribution and use. Furthermore, there is nothing in the Chafee exemption that requires the purchase of a print version of the textbook for students who are eligible for alternate-format versions, although in practice the print version is purchased as an artifact of a site's purchasing policies.

Finally, as these localized accessible-format creation efforts become more widespread, the determination of which students are actually eligible to receive these versions is often left to special education personnel, who may or may not be fully aware of the constraints imposed by the Chafee exemption. Even when special educators are aware of the requirements however, the division of students into "haves" and "have-nots" may appear arbitrary and capricious, and fundamentally inequitable. Faced with providing only some students with accessible materials, most educators will decide to support the equal-access provisions of federal special education and disabilities law instead of abiding by copyright constraints. This, in turn, often begs the question of why these materials should not be made available to students who can certainly benefit from them, but who fall well outside the population sanctioned by Chafee (English-language learners, for example).

This cluster of challenges—the cost to publishers of responding to a myriad of state requirements with no compensation, the widespread increase in unmonitored localized solutions that may negatively impact textbook sales, and increased pressure to extend the provision of these materials to an ever-widening circle of students—poses a significant challenge to the creation of a commercial solution.

A commercial solution offers one of the most compelling scenarios for the timely provision of high-quality accessible textbooks to students with or without print disabilities. Many textbook publishers are now routinely acquiring the rights to reproduce materials digitally as well as in print. If states, districts, schools, and classrooms were willing to purchase these materials in addition to or as an alternative to traditional print textbooks, it would eliminate the need to perpetuate ad hoc local solutions. Accessible commercial versions of textbooks could benefit from cooperative arrangements between existing third-party alternate-format conversion organizations—experts in designing materials to meet the needs of their constituents—and commercial publishers, who themselves would be motivated to invest in research and development to ensure the high quality of these products. In order for commercial publishers to envision the viability of this type of "market" solution, however, they will need to perceive the willingness of states, districts, and schools to purchase these materials.

ADJUSTMENTS BY EACH STAKEHOLDER GROUP WILL BENEFIT ALL

In order to address each of the three challenges listed above—technological, legislative, and commercial—each stakeholder group will be required to shift and adapt its current practice.

Publishers

Textbook publishers will need to develop the capacity to create properly formatted XML files. Some of the major publishing houses have already or are in the process of migrating to a digital (XML) workflow, and for these companies the creation of the agreed-upon source files will be an extension of an existing process. For publishers who do not have XML file creation capabilities, or for whom that process would be cost prohibitive (smaller, supplemental publishers, for example), the creation of these files will be more problematic and will likely require new and innovative partnerships. All publishers will need to be provided with technical assistance, guidelines, and models in order for them to create valid and properly structured XML files. Finally, publishers will need to be convinced that the technological investment will contain their current costs, facilitate their ability to respond to multiple state and local requirements, maintain quality, and align with intellectual property law.

Third-Party Conversion Organizations

Existing "Chafee-compliant" nonprofit alternate-format conversion organizations like Recording for the Blind and Dyslexic, BookShare, American Printing House for the Blind, and others will need to envision strategic partnerships that place their expertise at the beginning of a publisher's product cycle, rather than just at the end of it. If publishers produce only print-based materials, then the primary work of third-party organizations is the transformation of those print works into accessible formats. Once publishers are able to produce digital files routinely, however, the need for third-party conversion will diminish incrementally, while the opportunity to incorporate accommodations and alternatives directly into curriculum materials—a universal design approach—will increase concomitantly. A collaborative approach, pairing the disability and alternate-format expertise of the third-party conversion organizations with the editorial and instructional expertise of curriculum publishers, will likely result in more innovative and accessible products than either organization could create independently.

States, Districts, and Schools

Educators who teach and support students with disabilities will need to assess the benefits of embracing a more proactive and systemic approach to acquiring alternate-format materials for their students. While existing district or school-level solutions may address the immediate needs of individual students, in most instances these solutions are neither scalable not cost efficient. They often yield curriculum materials of inferior quality, and in some circumstances, these initiatives may violate copyright law. Furthermore, and perhaps of most importance, these local content transformation efforts divert the efforts of education personnel from the process of instruction.

States that have enacted accessible-textbook legislation (braille and beyond) are also most likely to have established centralized accessible-textbook distribution systems to support those mandates. The purpose of these centralized approaches is to ensure copyright compliance, quality, and timeliness, and to minimize redundancy and inefficiency. In many circumstances, the management and oversight of these systems by states also frees district and school education personnel from the process of retrofitting materials and allows them to redirect their time to instruction.

To further institutionalize the expectation that students with print disabilities will be provided with accessible and appropriate alternate-format versions, some states have added an additional consideration to their Individual Education Plan (IEP) and Section 505 Plan documents. Asking the site-based teams who know the needs of individual students best to document whether or not the student is eligible to receive accessible alternate-format curriculum materials reinforces the expectation that these materials will be provided.

Finally, as the requests (or in some cases, the requirements) for accessible materials from states, districts, and schools increase, these entities need to express their willingness to purchase these products. Textbooks and associated instructional materials can be made accessible by design, and the availability of these versions as market alternatives will only occur if the market is perceived as viable.

ACCESSIBLE TEXTBOOKS: REACHING EVERY STUDENT, THEN TEACHING EVERY STUDENT

While the primary purpose of establishing either a national alternate-format distribution process or a market-based solution is to ensure the timely provision of accessible materials to students with disabilities, it is important to keep in mind the goal that these materials are intended to support the education of these students. From that perspective, it is necessary to address how, and to what extent, alternate, accessible versions of textbooks enhance student achievement. This emphasis on increasing the achievement of all students, including those with disabilities and other learning needs, is a hallmark of NCLB, and needs to be an active consideration as accessible, alternate format materials become more widely available.

The existing NIMAS initiative is developing within the constraints imposed by existing copyright law, and the Section 121 exemption (Chafee Amendment) that addresses the needs of a specific subset of students with print disabilities. As referenced in the NIMAS Version 1.0 report:

> Students who manifest a print disability as the result of a physical or sensory impairment (blind, low-vision and some learning disabled students) currently qualify, while students who may struggle equally to decipher or extract meaning from print (ADHD, deaf and hard of hearing, students with limited cognitive of abilities, etc.) do not. (National File Format Technical Panel, 2004)

Regardless of which students are presently eligible to receive alternate-format textbooks, the fact remains that the precedent-setting consensus-building achieved by the National File Format Technical Panel has established both a foundation for the creation of accessible, alternate-format versions and the broad-based momentum necessary to deliver these versions to students who require them. In addition to the states (Kentucky, Arizona, New Mexico) that have already referenced the adoption of NIMAS in their statewide accessible-textbook legislation, major publishing houses (Thomson, Pearson, Houghton Mifflin, McGraw-Hill) have pledged NIMAS adoption as well. Furthermore, major postsecondary publishers and a number of organizations working to secure accessible versions of college textbooks have indicated that they will adopt the NIMAS standard, once formalized, in their procurement processes.

This momentum toward a standardized approach raises a significant question: since accessible versions of core curriculum print textbooks, both for students with disabilities and those without, have previously not been available in sufficient quantities to measure their broad impact within the context of academic achievement, what impact do they have? Data in the NIMAS Version 1.0 report provide some documentation to support the conclusion that students with a wide range of disabilities (including those who currently qualify as persons with print disabilities and those who do not) can benefit from technology-based instructional solutions.

An extensive summary of research in this area has been prepared by the National Center on Accessing the General Curriculum (Strangman, Hall, & Meyer, 2003). Among many studies in this area are the following:

- Students with language-related disabilities showed positive effects for word recognition, comprehension, and fluency when using digital texts with syllable- or letter-name-level synthetic speech transformations (Elbro, Rasmussen, & Spelling, 1996).
- Students with attentional, organizational, and learning disabilities showed increased academic gain when exposed to technology-supported concept mapping strategies (Anderson-Inman, Knox-Quinn, & Horney, 1996; Herl, O'Neil, Chung, & Schacter, 1999).
- Students who are deaf or hard of hearing showed consistent academic gains when provided with the sequential text highlighting and supportive captions available in digital instructional materials (McInerney, Riley, & Osher, 1999; Andrews & Jordan, 1997).
- Students with low cognitive abilities demonstrated increased functional skills when exposed to flexible technologies that maximized their strengths while helping to compensate for their weaknesses (Wehmeyer, Smith, Palmer, Davies, & Stock, 2003; Carroll, 1993).

We know that visually impaired students cannot see words or images, and that alternate-format versions of text, specifically digital, can more easily be converted to braille or voice with text descriptions of images. Students who cannot hold a print book or turn its pages can turn the virtual "pages" of a digital book with a key press or a switch. Students who cannot decode the text can benefit from having words read aloud by a computer. Going beyond baseline accessibility, students who lack background vocabulary can benefit from definitions (in English or another language) that can be readily provided. Digital texts can also be embedded with supports for syntax, semantics, and comprehension (Boone & Higgins, 1993; Dalton, Pisha, Eagleton, Coyne, & Deysher, 2001; MacArthur & Haynes, 1995).

The advantage of digital source files is that these and many other alternatives can be created from them and made available on an individual-student basis. These versions then become available for students who require them and, ultimately, became an option for students who may prefer them. They enable teachers to individualize materials in previously unimaginable ways (Hay, 1997; Lewin, 2000; MacArthur & Haynes, 1995). Customized alternatives can substantially reduce the barriers found in traditional texts; research evidence demonstrates the benefits of using such digital materials in the classroom (Barker & Torgesen, 1995; Bottge, 1999; Dalton et al., 2001; Erdner, Guy, & Bush, 1998; MacArthur & Haynes, 1995; Wise, Ring, & Olson, 1999).

CONCLUSION

Technological advances during the past fifty years have resulted in alternate-format materials, providing students with disabilities access to a world of information and ideas that traditionally has been restricted to printed text. Consistent braille formatting, high-quality audio versions, synthetic speech, and electronic text are just some examples. Because it offers significantly increased flexibility and enables rapid transformations from one media type to another, electronic text in particular is emerging as the foundation of a revolutionary approach to the provision of alternate-format materials. As that approach is realized, students with disabilities will be provided with a wide range of accessible and individualized learning materials—materials that have been extracted from a single digital source file. The efficiency of this approach is immediately apparent, and while there are numerous legal, commercial, and technological issues to overcome, everyone stands to gain from achieving a solution.

REFERENCES

Abell, M., Bauder, D., & Simmons, T. (2004). Universally designed online assessment: Implications for the future. *Information Technology and Disabilities, 10*(1).

Adler, A. (2002). *AAP's perspective on accessible curriculum materials for K–12 classrooms.* Available from http://www.cast.org/publications/ncac/ncac_policy.html

American Foundation for the Blind. (2003). *State braille laws.* Retrieved March, 2006, from http://www.tsbvi.edu/textbooks/afb/state-laws.htm

Anderson-Inman, L., Knox-Quinn, C., & Horney, M. A. (1996). Computer-based study strategies for students with learning disabilities: Individual differences associated with adoption level. *Journal of Learning Disabilities, 29,* 461–484.

Andrews, J., & Jordan, D. (1997). Multimedia, language learning, and Hispanic-deaf students. In R. Rittenhouse & D. Spillers (Eds.), *The electronic classroom: Helping teachers enhance the curriculum for students*. Little Rock: University of Arkansas Press.

Barker, T. A., & Torgesen, J. K. (1995). An evaluation of computer-assisted instruction in phonological awareness with below average readers. *Journal of Educational Computing Research, 13*(1), 89–103.

Beirne-Smith, M., Ittenbach, R., & Patton, J. R. (1998). *Mental retardation* (5th ed.). Upper Saddle River, NJ: Prentice Hall.

Boone, R., & Higgins, K. (1993). Hypermedia basal readers: Three years of school-based research. *Journal of Special Education Technology, 7*(2), 86–106.

Bottge, B. (1999). Effects of contextualized math instruction on problem solving of average and below-average achieving students. *Journal of Special Education, 33*(2), 81–92.

Bowe, F. (1999). *Universal design in education: Teaching non-traditional students*. Westport, CT: Greenwood Press.

Carroll, J. B. (1993). *Human cognitive abilities: A survey of factor-analytical studies*. New York: Cambridge University Press.

Dalton, B. (2003, Spring). Universal learning environments: Closing the gap for struggling readers and at-risk students. *Technology in Literacy Resource, 4*. Available from http://donjohnston.co.uk/newsletters

Dalton, B., Pisha, B., Eagleton, M., Coyne, P., & Deysher, S. (2001). *Engaging the text: Reciprocal teaching and questioning strategies in a scaffolded learning environment* (Final report to the U.S. Office of Special Education). Peabody, MA: CAST.

Dolan, R. P., & Hall, T. E. (2001). Universal design for learning: Implications for large-scale assessment. *IDA Perspectives, 27*(4), 22–25.

Dolan, R. P., & Hall, T. E. (2003). *Providing a read-aloud accommodation without compromising student independence: Preliminary results from a pilot study to evaluate the role of digital technologies in supporting universally designed large-scale assessments*. Wakefield, MA: CAST.

Edyburn, D. L. (2004). Measuring assistive technology outcomes in reading. *Journal of Special Education Technology, 19*(1). Available from http://jset.unlv.edu/19.1/asseds/edyburn.html

Elbro, C., Rasmussen, I., & Spelling, B. (1996). Teaching reading to disabled readers with language disorders: A controlled evaluation of synthetic speech feedback. *Scandinavian Journal of Psychology, 37*, 140–155.

Ellis, E. (1997). Watering up the curriculum for adolescents with learning disabilities: Goals of the knowledge dimension. *Remedial and Special Education, 18*, 326–346.

Ellis, E. S., & Sabornie, E. J. (1990). Strategy-based adaptive instruction in content-area classes: Social validity of six options. *Teacher Education and Special Education, 13*, 133–144.

Elmore, R. F., & Fuhrman, S. H. (1995). Opportunity-to-learn standards and the state role in education. *Teachers College Record, 96*, 433–458.

Erdner, R. A., Guy, R. F., & Bush, A. (1998). The impact of a year of computer assisted instruction on the development of first grade learning skills. *Journal of Educational Computing Research, 18*, 369–386.

Gloeckler, L. (2001). The door to opportunity: Let's open it for everyone. *State Education Standard, 2*(3), 20–25.

Gordon, D. T. (2002). Curriculum access in the digital age: New technology-based strategies offer hope that students of all abilities will have the opportunity to thrive in school. *Harvard Education Letter, 18*(1), 1–5.

Guiton, G., & Oakes, J. (1995). Opportunity to learn and conceptions of educational equality. *Educational Evaluation and Policy Analysis, 17*, 323–336.

Gurry, S., & Larkin, A. (1999). Literacy learning abilities of children with developmental disabilities: What do we know? *Currents in Literacy, 2*(1). Available from http://www.lesley.edu/academic_centers/hood/currentshome.html

Hay, L. (1997). Tailor-made instructional materials using computer multimedia technology. *Computers in the Schools, 13*(1–2), 61–68.

Herl, H. E., O'Neil, H. F., Jr., Chung, G. K. W. K., & Schacter, J. (1999). Reliability and validity of a computer-based knowledge mapping system to measure content understanding. *Computers in Human Behavior, 15*, 315–333.

Hickson, L., Blackman, L. S., & Reis, E. M. (1995). *Mental retardation: Foundations of educational programming.* Boston: Allyn & Bacon.

Holt, J. A., Traxler, C. B., & Allen, T. E. (1997). *Interpreting the scores: A user's guide to the 9th edition Stanford Achievement Test for educators of deaf and hard-of-hearing students* (Gallaudet Research Institute Technical Report 97-1). Washington, DC: Gallaudet University.

Hudson, S. B., McMahon, K. C., & Overstreet, C. M. (2002). *The 2000 National Survey of Science and Mathematics Education: Compendium of tables.* Chapel Hill, NC: Horizon Research.

Koppenhaver, D. A., Erickson, K. A., & Skotko, B. G. (2001). Supporting communication of girls with Rett syndrome and their mothers in storybook reading. *International Journal of Disability, Development, and Education, 48*, 395–410.

Levine, P., & Wagner, M. (2004). *Secondary school students' experiences in special education classrooms* (National Longitudinal Transition Study-2). Menlo Park, CA: SRI.

Lewin, C. (2000). Exploring the effects of talking book software in U.K. primary classrooms. *Journal of Research in Reading, 23*, 149–157.

MacArthur, C. A., & Haynes, J. B. (1995). Student Assistant for Learning from Text (SALT): A hypermedia reading aid. *Journal of Learning Disabilities, 28*(3), 50–59.

McCarthy, B. (2002, June 28). *The Instructional Materials Accessibility Act: Making materials available to all students.* Testimony before the Health, Education, Labor, and Pensions Committee, United States Senate hearing on S.2246. Retrieved August 2006 from http://www.afb.org/section.asp?SECTIONID=49&TopicID=258&DocumentID=1772

McDonnell, L., McLaughlin, M., & Morison, P. (1997). *Educating one and all: Students with disabilities in standards-based reform.* Washington, DC: National Academy Press.

McInerney, M., Riley, K., & Osher, D. (1999). *Technology to support literacy strategies for students who are deaf.* Washington, DC: American Institutes for Research.

Moon, T. R., Callahan, C. M., & Tomlinson, C. A. (1999). The effects of mentoring relationships on preservice teachers' attitudes toward academically diverse students. *Gifted Child Quarterly, 43*(2), 56–62.

National Center for Education Statistics. (2002). *Digest of education statistics.* Washington, DC: U.S. Department of Education.

National File Format Technical Panel. (2004, July). *National instructional materials accessibility standard report—version 1.0.* Wakefield, MA: National Center on Accessing the General Curriculum. Retrieved March, 2006, from http://www.cast.org/ncac/nimas/executive_summary.htm

National Reading Panel. (2000). *Teaching children to read: An evidence-based assessment of the scientific research literature on reading and its implications for reading instruction.* Bethesda, MD: National Institute of Child Health and Human Development.

North Central Regional Education Laboratory. (2002). *Exemplary reading programs in Illinois public schools: Critical features of successful reading programs.* Retrieved March, 2006 from http://www.ncrel.org/sdrs/areas/isbe/isbecrit.htm

Orkwis, R. (1999). *Curriculum access and universal design for learning* (ERIC/OSEP Digest #E586). Reston, VA: ERIC Clearinghouse on Disabilities and Gifted Education. Available from http://www.ericdigests.org/2000-4/access.htm

Orkwis, R. (2003). *Universally designed instruction* (ERIC/OSEP Digest). Reston, VA: ERIC Clearinghouse on Disabilities and Gifted Education. Available from http://www.ericdigests.org/2003-5/universally.htm

Padden, C., & Ramsey, C. (1998). Reading ability in signing Deaf children. *Topics in Language Disorders, 18*(4), 30–46.

Perl, E. S. (2002). *Federal and state legislation regarding accessible instructional materials.* Available from http://www.cast.org/publications/ncac/ncac_policy.html

Perl, E. S., & Gordon, D. (2003). *U.S. states and territories accessible curriculum survey.* Wakefield, MA: NCAC Policy Development Group/Harvard Children's Initiative. Available from http://nimas.cast.org/about/resources/statessurvey.html

Peter Li Education Group. (2002). A profile of the site-based public and private school market. *2002 Today's School Survey.* Available from http://www.peterli.com/ts/resources/rptsts.shtm

Prinz, P., & Strong, M. (1998). ASL proficiency and English literacy within a bilingual Deaf education model of instruction. *Topics in Language Disorders, 18*(4), 47–60.

Ravitch, D. (2000). *The reauthorization of the federal Elementary and Secondary Education Act: An introduction* (Brookings Papers on Educational Policy). Washington, DC: Brookings Institution Press.

Roblin, J. (1993). *The reading fingers: The life of Louis Braille* (R. G. Mandalian, Trans.). New York: American Foundation for the Blind. (Original work published 1952)

Rose, D. H., & Meyer, A. (2002). *Teaching every student in the digital age: Universal design for learning.* Alexandria, VA: Association for Supervision and Curriculum Development.

Strong, M., & Prinz, P. (1997). A study of the relationship between American Sign Language and English literacy. *Journal of Deaf Studies and Deaf Education, 2*(1), 37–46.

Thompson, S., & Thurlow, M. (2002). *Universally designed assessments: Better tests for everyone!* (Policy Directions No. 14). Minneapolis: University of Minnesota, National Center on Educational Outcomes. Retrieved September 15, 2004, from http://education.umn.edu/NCEO/OnlinePubs/Policy14.htm

Thurlow, M. (2002). Positive educational results for all students: The promise of standards based reform. *Remedial and Special Education, 23,* 195–202.

Wehmeyer, M., Smith, S. J., Palmer, S., Davies, D., & Stock, S. (2003). Technology use and people with mental retardation. In L. M. Glidden (Ed.), *International review of research in mental retardation.* San Diego: Academic Press.

Wise, B. W., Ring, J., & Olson, R. K. (1999). Training phonological awareness with and without explicit attention to articulation. *Journal of Experimental Child Psychology, 72,* 271–304.

Note: This report was written with support from the National Center on Accessing the General Curriculum, a cooperative agreement between CAST and the U.S. Department of Education, Office of Special Education Programs, Cooperative Agreement No. H324H990004. The opinions expressed herein do not necessarily reflect the policy or position of the U.S. Department of Education, Office of Special Education Programs, and no official endorsement by the department should be inferred. This work was also supported through a subcontract agreement with the Access Center: Improving Outcomes for All Student K–8 at the American Institutes for Research. The Access Center is funded by the U.S. Department of Education, Office of Special Education Programs, Cooperative Agreement #H326K02003.

CHAPTER TEN

Engaging the Text: Brain Research and the Universal Design of Reading Strategy Supports

DAVID H. ROSE AND BRIDGET DALTON

READING AND THE BRAIN

The last decade of the twentieth century brought a wealth of new insights in the neurosciences. Much of this was due to new technologies that revolutionized the way we can study the learning brain. Formerly, most of our knowledge of the human brain came from postmortem studies of individuals with brain damage. Now, new imaging technologies like positron emission tomography (PET) and functional magnetic resonance imaging (fMRI) allow us to look into active, living, learning brains without damaging them. Using computers, we can view patterns of activity as images, as in Figure 1. These images show "hot spots," areas of intense brain activity, providing a window into the learning brain and offering insight into a broad range of behaviors, including reading.

Reading Is Distributed in the Brain

What have we learned from brain imaging? First, we have learned that brain activity is distributed: different regions of the brain carry out different aspects of learning (just as specialists carry out different elements of movie production: "Color by Technicolor" and "Dolby Sound"). Each of these regions is specialized for a particular task. The overall effect is rather like that of a well-organized committee or work group, where each member's special skills contribute to the group's overall success. The sum is often greater than its parts.

For example, studies have shown that when a person views an image, its various features, such as color, shape, and orientation are processed in different regions of the brain. This separate but simultaneous processing of different characteristics of an image by highly specialized regions enables us to recognize images quickly and efficiently. The combined effect of these "specialists" working together is the creation of something very complex in a short amount of time.

Distributed processing has some important implications for cognitive constructions like reading comprehension and language. Reading comprehension and language are composed of many component processes that are distributed throughout the brain. Although conceptually we tend to lump them together, the brain does not. As an example, see Figure 2.

All four of these images show brain activity during the performance of a language task, but the specific demands of each task are different, and thus so are the regions of the brain involved. This suggests that there is no single language center in the brain, but instead there are many regions that contribute to normal language facility. Different regions are recruited depending on the specific demands of the language task.

What does this say about reading comprehension? First, comprehension is likely to be an amalgam of many component processes, rather than a single process. There are likely different ways of comprehending, reflected by different patterns of processing in the brain. A study by Nichelli, Grafman, Pietrini, Clark, Lee, and Miletich (1995), for example, showed that reading elicits different patterns of activity in the brain, depending upon the nature of the reading instructions. When researchers asked subjects to read the same text (an Aesop's fable) four times, but with different reading instructions each time, the brain evidenced different patterns of activity during each reading. The response of the brain was influenced by the reader's purpose in comprehending the text.

FIGURE 1   Computer Images Depicting Brain Activity: Hearing Words and Seeing Words (Highly active brain regions appear as hot spots on the images.)

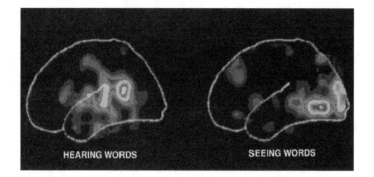

Source: Petersen, Fox, Posner, Mintun, and Raichle (1988). Reprinted with permission from *Nature.*
Copyright © 1988 Macmillan Magazines Limited.

FIGURE 2   Computer Images Depicting Average Brain Activity: Performing Four Language Tasks

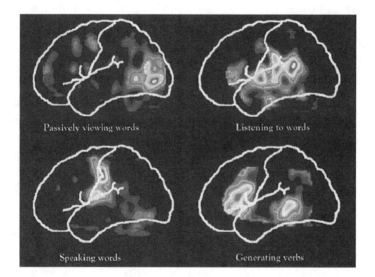

Source: Petersen, Fox, Posner, Mintun, and Raichle (1988). Reprinted with permission from *Nature.*
Copyright © 1988 Macmillan Magazines Limited.

Brain studies reveal that reading comprehension, like other cognitive activities, is probably a highly differentiated and distributed activity.

Individual Differences and Learning in the Brain

Brain images show that the distribution of hot spots varies across individuals; when different individuals perform the same task, somewhat different regions of the brain are active. While the overall patterns of activity are the same, there are consistent and compelling individual differences.

One illustrative study of individual differences in reading was performed by Shaywitz, Shaywitz, Pugh, and colleagues (1998). They compared the brain activity of individuals with and without dyslexia-type reading disabilities during reading.

Note that in Figure 3, the brain activity of the dyslexic readers is heavily concentrated in the frontal brain regions, while the brain activity of the other reader is more distributed and includes posterior portions of the brain. It does not appear (as many mistakenly believe) that dyslexic individuals are "not trying." It seems more likely that they are trying quite hard, but that their brains are working in very different ways. This study, and many others, makes it clear that reading-related brain activity varies from person to person.

Experience Shapes Reading-Related Brain Activity

Another source of variance in brain activity is related to time and experience. One of the most unremarkable and yet totally surprising findings of recent brain imaging studies is that the brain changes when it learns. The changes that brain imaging makes visible are different from those that are apparent at the anatomical and chemical levels. The images show a changing distribution of brain activity over time.

The first two images in Figure 4 show brain activity recorded from a subject performing a verb generation task (the subject was presented with a noun and asked to generate an associated verb). There is a striking change from the first image to the second image. The second image shows brain activity during performance of exactly the same task but after significant learning has occurred through repeated trials. Follow-

FIGURE 3   Brain Activity of Individuals with and without Dyslexia Reading

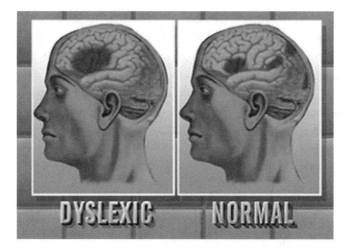

Source: Ponce (1998). Used by permission of *Online NewsHour.*

FIGURE 4   Computer Images Depicting Brain Activity: Changes Due to Experience

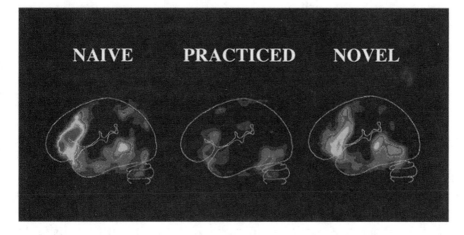

Source: Adapted from Raichle, Fiez, Videen, MacLeod, Pardo, Fox, and Petersen (1994), by permission of Oxford University Press.

ing practice, there is a huge reduction, or savings, in activity—the brain shows less activity once it is practiced with the task. In the third image, renewed activity is observable, the result of slight changes in the task that require renewed effort by the performer. But the activity is still less than it was to begin with—indicating that there is considerable transfer of practice from the first task to the second task.

Many studies have repeated this pattern of findings: the brain exhibits tremendous activity at the beginning of a task, when it is unskilled. Later, as learning occurs, brain activity is redistributed or reduced. In short, the unskilled brain shows a very different distribution of activity from the skilled one. At least one neuroscientist has described this pattern as scaffolding; multiple brain regions are recruited to perform new and unstructured tasks (Petersen, van Mier, Fiez, & Raichle, 1998).

To summarize, any complicated activity like reading comprehension requires a highly distributed set of processors in the brain. The distribution can be quite variable, and depends on the specific nature of the task, on the specific nature of the individual, and on what learning has already occurred. (Other factors can also make a difference in which areas of the brain are active—including brain injury and sex differences, for example—but they are beyond the scope of this chapter.)

The next section briefly describes three broad regions of the brain that we call recognition, strategic, and affective networks involved in learning. These three networks are specialized in very different ways, but all three have an integral role in reading comprehension.

THREE BROAD NETWORKS FOR LEARNING

Reading Comprehension and Recognition Networks

The back half of the brain's cerebral hemispheres consists of giant networks of neurons that receive input from the various sensory organs (the eyes and ears, for example) and use it to construct meaning. These recognition networks make it possible to recognize a particular pattern of input as a cup, a dog, grandmother's voice, or the smell of coffee. In reading, these networks play a fundamental role in recognizing the many patterns in text: recognizing that the letters c-a-t are a unique pattern that stands for the word *cat*, recognizing the silent *e* pattern in spelling, identifying a particular pattern of words as a sonnet or a haiku, and recognizing a particular arrangement of words as William Faulkner's style.

Damage to the posterior recognition networks can impair the brain's ability to recognize things. At the extreme are individuals who, because of injury or illness, can no longer recognize once-familiar people by their faces or the distinctive sounds of a classical symphony. Damage to these networks can also impair reading ability, since many aspects of reading also depend on intact pattern recognition.

Reading Comprehension and Strategic Networks

In the front half of the cerebral hemispheres are networks that are specialized for entirely different functions. These networks are specialized to construct and transmit patterns of output; they are involved in making skillful patterns of action and knowing how to do things, like taking steps, saying words, shooting a foul shot, reading a book, driving a car, planning a vacation, or writing a narrative. All of our skills, strategies, and plans are essentially highly patterned actions.

Damage to these strategic networks interferes with generating successful plans and actions. At one extreme are individuals who are paralyzed (unable to move voluntarily). At the other are individuals who are able to move easily but are unable to plan and coordinate their various activities effectively; they seem disorganized, impulsive, and uncoordinated.

Reading comprehension requires strategic networks as well as recognition networks. Understanding text is more than simply reception or perception; good readers approach text skillfully and strategically. They monitor their performance by making and testing predictions; they scan important pieces of text for salient information; they identify the overall structure of the text and draw inferences about meaning and motive; they analyze parts of words to hypothesize their meanings; and they re-read puzzling sentences. All of these reading comprehension skills depend upon strategic networks.

Reading Comprehension and Affective Networks

A third set of networks, the affective networks, is localized primarily in the central core of the brain. These networks are critical for emotions—fear, desire, sadness, excitement, and hope. They specialize not in recognizing or generating patterns, but in determining whether the patterns we perceive matter to us, thus helping us to decide which actions and strategies to pursue.

Impairments in affective networks distort the importance of various aspects of the world, thereby influencing our abilities to establish priorities, select what is valuable, focus attention, and choose actions. The ability to determine accurately the patterns that really count, to differentiate the important from the unimportant, is a third integral component to human intelligence.

Without well-functioning affective networks, reading comprehension is impaired. Readers are not able to direct and sustain attention to specific aspects of text. Nor are they able to focus appropriately on specific words or paragraphs that are important, or vary their style or rate to accommodate differences in content or purpose.

Recognition, strategic, and affective networks normally operate in concert as a distributed system. For example, recognition networks function to identify a particular pattern of shapes, colors, and smells as a hamburger. Strategic networks create plans and actions that allow us to walk over, reach out, lift, and munch on that hamburger. And affective networks motivate us, depending on our status in Weight Watchers points, either to approach or avoid that hamburger.

Implications for Reading Comprehension

Brain research emphasizes the varied and distributed nature of comprehension: comprehension is not a single activity, but is many processes distributed across different functional networks that operate in parallel. We have emphasized three broad networks that are all essential to comprehension. In unique ways, impairment in any of these networks can make readers vulnerable to reading failure: students may fail because they cannot recognize the relevant patterns in text, because they lack strategies for constructing meaning from text, or because they do not find reading important enough to sustain the effort it demands.

Brain research also emphasizes that the fundamental processes underlying reading comprehension differ among individuals in nontrivial ways. Individuals do not differ in some generalized or simply quantifiable way (like a global intelligence score), but in many specific ways. Intelligence is the product of networks of processes, any element of which may be different in two individuals.

Learning is marked by qualitative changes in the kinds of processors that are engaged. Early learning activates a spatially and anatomically distinctive array of brain structures, often more expansive than those that are activated by later learning or mastery.

Do these broad generalizations about these three functional networks enlighten us as we think about comprehension? Let us look again at Figure 3, which compares dyslexic and normal readers. It is now clear not only that the dyslexic population displaying a pattern that is distributed differently from the nondyslexic population, but also that the dyslexic readers are expending most of their energy within the strategic networks. What does that mean?

Certainly more research is needed to know for certain, but it is apparent that this pattern is similar to that observed for beginning or unskilled students in other research. The students with dyslexia are reading words with the front part of the brain, effortfully and strategically. Other readers are more automatic, recognizing the patterns in the words easily, with little effort. Unfortunately, the allocation of effort to sound out the words strategically must come at the cost of allocating that same effort to monitoring comprehension strategically. Thus, like the beginning reader, the reader with dyslexia requires a lot of scaffolding, from internal or external resources, in order to comprehend adequately. That scaffolding can come from skillful use of the brain's internal scaffolding processes, from a willing tutor, or from a peer who is reading collaboratively. Until now, it has been difficult to find that scaffolding within the text itself. But as we shall see, that is changing.

THE ENGAGING THE TEXT PROJECT: USING TECHNOLOGY TO DEVELOP SUPPORTED READING ENVIRONMENTS

Reading instruction is evolving to offer the kinds of scaffolding that readers need to overcome weaknesses in any of the three networks that we have described. In ongoing research, we are applying recent advances in brain research and reading comprehension research on strategy instruction (Palincsar & Brown, 1984; Pressley, 2000) to the design of computer-supported reading environments.

Comprehension of a particular text is the result of an interaction, or transaction, between the reader, the text, the purpose for reading, and in school, the instructional context (Lipson & Wixson, 1997). Reading is a complex cognitive process that is socially based and constructed. It is also a thinking process, and skilled readers actively construct meaning as they read. To succeed with such a multifaceted and challenging task, learners need highly effective instruction. In the Engaging the Text Project (Dalton, Pisha, Eagleton, Coyne, & Deysher, 2002), we have been working with middle school teachers to study the effects of computer-supported strategy instruction on struggling readers' comprehension. Most of the students in the study have been identified as having learning disabilities and are typically reading three to four grade levels below placement. These students struggle to decode and may never develop the automatic word recognition essential to fluent reading and text comprehension (Ehri, 1994). Many also have difficulty reading for meaning, monitoring their comprehension, and taking action when they don't understand (Lipson & Wixson, 1997).

As a result of these struggles, books and other texts that constitute the general curriculum function as barriers rather than gateways for learning for these students. Decoding difficulties block students from access to important content, and comprehension problems block them from responding to and learning from text in meaningful ways. For many students, these difficulties contribute to low self-efficacy and a feeling that applying effort will not result in a positive outcome (Guthrie, 2001). Some invest their energy in compensating for their difficulties, while others disengage from literacy and other academic tasks, or act out. For these students, the consequences can be severe, given the climate of high stakes testing in many states. Already, results show that a significant number of students are not passing basic competency exams (Massachusetts Department of Education, 2000).

How can reading comprehension instruction be made more effective? A wealth of research evidence over the last twenty years strongly supports the teaching of reading comprehension strategies (for recent reviews of this literature, see National Reading Panel, 2000; Pressley, 2000; Rosenshine & Meister, 1994; for a review of this literature for students with learning disabilities, see Swanson, 1999). The most commonly used strategies are making predictions, questioning, summarizing, and clarifying. Visualization and graphic organizers are also often included in strategy instruction, as well as strategies for self-monitoring and evaluation. The general consensus is that "comprehension instruction can effectively motivate and teach readers to learn and to use comprehension strategies that benefit the reader" (National Reading Panel, 2000, pp. 4–6) and that multiple-strategy instruction carried out in natural classroom settings is more beneficial than the teaching of individual strategies.

The Engaging the Text Project uses hypertext Web links to deliver a supported reading comprehension environment that includes interactivity and multimedia. Research on students' comprehension in hypertext is somewhat limited, but the results are promising (for a review, see Kamil, Intrator, & Kim, 2000). Studies indicate that students with learning disabilities benefit from supports such as vocabulary definitions (MacArthur & Haynes, 1995) and anaphoric reference (Boone and Higgins, 1993), but students do not always access the supports that they need. The work of Anderson-Inman and her colleagues demonstrates that embedding tools and supports in hypertext can improve achievement if the tools are pedagogically sound and an instructor teaches students how to use them (Anderson-Inman, Knox-Quinn, & Horney, 1996; Anderson-Inman & Horney, 1997; Anderson-Inman & Zeitz, 1993).

The Engaging the Text Project is applying research-based strategy instruction to digital text. It is grounded in Universal Design for Learning theory (Meyer & Rose, 1998, 2000; Rose & Meyer, 2002). Universal Design for Learning focuses on the need for instructional methods and materials that provide students with a flexible system of supports for both access and learning. When we consider this approach to reading comprehension instruction in relation to what we know about learning, reading comprehension, and the brain, Universal Design for Learning offers reading experiences that flexibly support or scaffold students' diverse recognition, strategic, and affective networks. Scaffolding is central to this instructional approach and fits well with Vygotsky's (1978) con-

FIGURE 5   The Thinking Reader prototype is a computer-supported reading environment that embeds support for decoding and comprehension strategies in digital text.

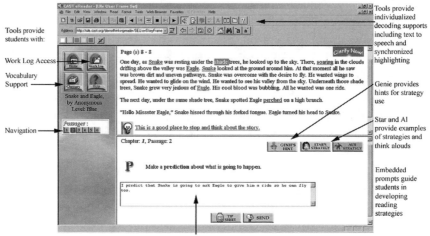

Tools provide students with:

Work Log Access

Vocabulary Support

Navigation

Tools provide individualized decoding supports including text to speech and synchronized highlighting

Genie provides hints for strategy use

Star and Al provide examples of strategies and think alouds

Embedded prompts guide students in developing reading strategies

Work space for student responses that are sent to work log

cept of the zone of proximal development. Learning takes place within this zone, where challenge and support are in balance so that the learner is able to achieve success and increase mastery.

We designed a research prototype CD-ROM that embeds strategy instruction within digitized novels. The prototype embodies the UDL perspective, providing supports to scaffold students' diverse recognition, strategic, and affective networks. Figure 5 presents a screen shot from the prototype. The following classroom scenario illustrates how the tool is being used to develop students who not only read for understanding, but are strategic and engaged readers.

Classroom Scenario

Derek, a sixth-grade student who reads on the third-grade level, is seated at the computer with headphones on, reading a digital version of *Hatchet* (Paulsen, 1987), an award-winning novel that is required by his school district. He clicks on a read-aloud button to have the text read to him. He encounters an unknown word, *wilderness*, and clicks on it to obtain a definition from the glossary. As he continues reading, the program occasionally prompts him to stop and think about the story and to use one of the strategies he has learned, such as predicting, questioning, clarifying, and summarizing.

Summary-writing is somewhat difficult for Derek, so he clicks on the strategy hint button. A genie appears and offers one of several hints that are based on a rubric for good summary writing, such as "A good summary captures the gist, or most important information," or "Be sure to include the character and the problem in your summary." Derek writes his summary in the response box on screen and sends his work to be posted to his worklog. He logs off and joins his class in a brief discussion of the novel. His teacher asks: Do we need to clarify? Who can give me a summary of what just happened in the story? How do you think Brian is feeling right now? What do you predict will happen next? As students talk, they resolve a confusion about where Brian is flying for the summer, and predict that the plane might crash or that something will happen when Brian meets his father.

The following week, Derek and his teacher have a miniconference to review his worklog with all of his strategy responses. Derek has selected his best example of strategy use and identified a goal that he thinks he should work on for the next few weeks: using more descriptive words in his visualizations. He and his teacher decide that he is ready to move to a lower level of scaffolding, one that provides less structure and will help move him along toward more independent strategy use while he is reading. Derek's teacher takes note of the fact that Derek and many other students are not clear about the distinction between questioning and clarifying, and she decides to conduct a minilesson the next day, modeling how to use these strategies and guiding students as they practice applying them while reading.

At the end of the year, Derek and his teacher reflect on how he has changed as a reader. Derek is feeling more confident about his abilities as a reader because the read-aloud feature of the software allowed him to read the same novels that his classmates were reading and to focus on understanding rather than decoding. His growth as a reader is also demonstrated by his performance on the end-of-year standardized reading assessment, his willingness to participate in class discussions, and his new interest in adventure stories and the work of author Gary Paulsen.

This has been a successful year for Derek. It has also been a successful year for his teacher, who views the prototype as an important tool for differentiating instruction and addressing the diverse needs of her students. The software does not replace her as a teacher; it extends her capacity to reach all of her students and to teach more effectively.

The results of this research suggest the promise of developing computer-supported reading environments based on an understanding of recent research in the neurosciences on how the brain learns, as well as the extensive body of research on reading comprehension, strategy instruction, and engagement.

THREE RECOMMENDATIONS FOR THE FUTURE

As research in the neurosciences continues to reveal the structure of individual differences in learning, we need to apply those findings continually to the work of understanding individual differences in reading comprehension.

As research develops new reading technologies and digital texts that allow us to individualize the teaching of reading comprehension, we need to provide teachers with those technologies.

As classrooms increasingly have access to new technologies for supporting the teaching of reading comprehension, we need to ensure that support and instruction are embedded within these technologies to assist both teachers and students in learning to use them well.

REFERENCES

Anderson-Inman, L., & Horney, M. A. (1997). Electronic books for secondary students. *Journal of Adolescent & Adult Literacy, 40*, 486–491.

Anderson-Inman, L., Knox-Quinn, C., & Horney, M. A. (1996). Computer-based study strategies for students with learning disabilities: Individual differences associated with adoption level. *Journal of Learning Disabilities, 29*, 461–484.

Anderson-Inman, L., & Zeitz, L. (1993). Computer-based concept mapping: Active studying for active learners. *Computing Teacher, 21*(1), 6.

Boone, R., & Higgins, K. (1993). Hypermedia basal readers: Three years of school-based research. *Journal of Special Education Technology, 7*(2), 86–106.

Dalton, B., Pisha, B., Eagleton, M., Coyne, P., & Deysher, S. (2002). *Engaging the text: Final report to the U.S. Department of Education.* Peabody, MA: CAST.

Ehri, L. C. (1994). Development of the ability to read words: Update. In R. B. Ruddell & M. R. Ruddell (Eds.), *Theoretical models and processes of reading* (4th ed., pp. 323–358). Washington, DC: International Reading Association.

Guthrie, J. T. (2001). Contexts for engagement and motivation in reading. *Reading Online, 4*(8).

Kamil, M. L., Intrator, S. M., & Kim, H. S. (2000). The effects of other technologies on literacy and literacy learning. In M. L. Kamil & P. B. Mosenthal (Eds.), *Handbook of reading research* (Vol. 3, pp. 771–788). Mahwah, NJ: Lawrence Erlbaum.

Lipson, M. Y., & Wixson, K. K. (1997). *Assessment and instruction of reading and writing disability: An interactive approach* (2nd ed.). New York: Longman.

MacArthur, C. A., & Haynes, J. B. (1995). Student Assistant for Learning from Text (SALT): A hypermedia reading aid. *Journal of Learning Disabilities, 28*(3), 50–59.

Massachusetts Department of Education. (2000). *1999 Massachusetts Comprehensive Assessment System (MCAS) technical report.* Boston: Author.

Meyer, A., & Rose, D. H. (1998). *Learning to read in the computer age* (Vol. 3). Cambridge, MA: Brookline Books.

Meyer, A., & Rose, D. H. (2000). Universal design for individual differences. *Educational Leadership, 58*(3), 39–43.

National Reading Panel. (2000). *Teaching children to read: An evidence-based assessment of the scientific research literature on reading and its implications for reading instruction.* Washington, DC: National Institute of Child Health and Human Development.

Nichelli, P., Grafman, J., Pietrini, P., Clark, K., Lee, K. Y., & Miletich, R. (1995). Where the brain appreciates the moral of a story. *NeuroReport, 6,* 2309–2313.

Palincsar, A. S., & Brown, A. L. (1984). Reciprocal teaching of comprehension-fostering and comprehension-monitoring activities. *Cognition and Instruction, 1*(2), 117.

Paulsen, G. (1987). *Hatchet.* New York: Simon & Schuster.

Petersen, S. E., Fox, P. T., Posner, M. I., Mintun, M., & Raichle, M. E. (1988). Positron emission tomographic studies of the cortical anatomy of single-word processing. *Nature, 331,* 585–589.

Petersen, S. E., van Mier, H., Fiez, J. A., & Raichle, M. E. (1998). The effects of practice on the functional anatomy of task performance. *Proceedings of the National Academy of Sciences, USA, 95,* 853–860.

Ponce, P. (1998). *Unscrambling dyslexia* [Interview with Sally Shaywitz and Reid Lyon]. Retrieved January 25, 2006, from http://www.pbs.org/newshour/bb/science/jan-june 98/dyslexia_3-11.html

Pressley, M. (2000). What should comprehension instruction be the instruction of? In M. L. Kamil, P. B. Mosenthal, P. D. Pearson & R. Barr (Eds.), *Handbook of reading research* (Vol. III, p. 1010). Mahwah, NJ: Lawrence Erlbaum.

Raichle, M. E., Fiez, J. A., Videen, T. O., MacLeod, A. M., Pardo, J. V., Fox, P. T., et al. (1994). Practice-related changes in human brain functional anatomy during nonmotor learning. *Cerebral Cortex, 4*(1), 8–26.

Rose, D. H., & Meyer, A. (2002). *Teaching every student in the digital age: Universal design for learning.* Alexandria, VA: Association for Supervision and Curriculum Development.

Rosenshine, B., & Meister, C. (1994). Reciprocal teaching: A review of the research. *Review of Educational Research, 64,* 479–530.

Shaywitz, S. E., Shaywitz, B. A., Pugh, K. R., Fulbright, R. K., Constable, R. T., Mencl, W. E., Shankweiler, D. P., Liberman, A. M., Skudlarski, P., Fletcher, J. M., Katz, L., Marchione, K. E., Lacadie, C., Gatenby, C., & Gore, J. C. (1998). Functional disruption in the organization of the brain for reading in dyslexia. *Proceedings of the National Academy of Sciences, USA, 95,* 2636–2641.

Swanson, H. L. (1999). Reading research for students with LD: A meta-analysis of intervention outcomes. *Journal of Learning Disabilities, 32,* 504–532.

Vygotsky, L. S. (1978). *Mind and society: The development of higher mental processes.* Cambridge, MA: Harvard University Press.

CHAPTER ELEVEN

Teaching Internet Literacy Strategies: The Hero Inquiry Project

MAYA B. EAGLETON, KATHLEEN GUINEE, AND KAREN LANGLAIS

Navigating the Internet has become an essential literacy task for today's middle school students. The World Wide Web is a uniquely rich resource for authentic inquiry, but students must learn to orchestrate sophisticated strategies to become literate in this complex environment (Eagleton, 2002). Despite the fact that 71 percent of adult Web users experience frustration when searching, and that the average Internet user feels discouraged after only twelve minutes of searching (Dutton, 2001), standards at national, state, and local levels call for integrating modern technologies such as the Internet into the classroom. For example, the National Council of Teachers of English and the International Reading Association Standards for the English Language Arts state that middle school students should "conduct research on issues and interests by generating ideas and questions, and by posing problems" using "a variety of technological and information resources" (NCTE/IRA, 1996). With 99 percent of U.S. public schools reporting Internet access, 85 percent of those with high-speed Internet access (National Center for Education Statistics, 2002), many language arts teachers now have the resources to meet these standards. Although many middle schoolers may be fluent with word processing or instant messaging, we cannot assume that students know how to find information efficiently on the Internet, and students who cannot find relevant information quickly will be disadvantaged in today's information society (Leu, 2000).

To teach these critical skills, we designed a six-week Internet inquiry unit in which eighth graders were required to use both print and Internet resources to research a personal hero, and then present their findings via two formats of their choosing—for example, a slide show, a poster, or an impersonation. While numerous strategies and skills can be emphasized in project-based learning, we focused on the earlier stages of the inquiry process—on choosing topics, asking research questions, and selecting keywords. The later stages of the process—identifying relevant information, note-taking, synthesizing, and transforming ideas—were not the focus of this instructional intervention because they are similar for online and traditional library research. Karen Langlais, the third author, taught the unit to eight language arts classes over two grading periods, while the first two authors observed and collected data for a research study funded by the U.S. Department of Education, Office of Special Education Programs. The curriculum was based on Universal Design for Learning (Rose & Meyer, 2002), a philosophy that seeks to create tools and materials in which the content, means of expression, and balance of support and challenge are customizable to support individual learners. Although the original target population for our research was mainstreamed students with learning disabilities, we quickly discovered that the Internet inquiry process is a challenging literacy task for all middle school learners.

In this article, we describe the hero inquiry project in detail, so that readers may implement similar units of study in their classrooms. The 6-week project is based on 50-minute class periods with the first 5 minutes dedicated to goal-stating, brief assessments, and student questions; then 15 minutes of teaching, modeling, and/or review; 25 minutes of guided and/or independent practice; and 5 minutes at the end of the period for students to reflect on their progress. These guidelines were flexible, depending on the school calendar, computer availability, students' individual needs, and daily instructional objectives.

TABLE 1   Potential Formats for Presenting Research Findings

Print	Multimedia	Performance	Art
Newspaper article	Website	Skit	Diorama
Poem	Slide show	Mock interview	Captioned poster
Diary	Children's book	Impersonation	Board game
Opinion paper	Brochure	Song	Timeline
Essay	Video	Speech	Wanted poster

WEEK 1: INTRODUCTION

The first week was dedicated to setting goals, administering pretest assessments, brainstorming final formats (see Table 1), introducing tools (search engines, library resources), and exploring the hero theme. Discussing project objectives with students up front and having them set learning goals were crucial, although clear goals are essential for learning (Rose & Meyer, 2002) we have observed in previous (unpublished) pilot studies that many middle school students begin researching without explicit goals or strategies for approaching the task. We showed the eighth graders exactly how their work would be evaluated, using a grading rubric that allowed them to self-assess process, progress, and products (see Table 2). This grading system helped level the playing field for students with varying degrees of Internet inquiry expertise. The grading rubric not only helped students understand project objectives, but also gave them a framework for setting personal learning goals as well as an opportunity to assess their growth.

To find out what students already knew about searching the Internet, we asked them to list the steps involved in searching (see Figure 1), and then we observed some individual students as they carried out an Internet search for an unfamiliar subject. Example: "Imagine someone gave you a lory [a type of parrot] as a pet and you need to find information about it on the Internet. Show me how you would find the information that you would need, and talk through every step as you go so I can un-

TABLE 2   Partial Grading Rubric

	4	3	2	1	0	Student Score	Teacher Score
Process							
Classwork	I turned in every class assignment	I turned in most class assignments	I turned in some class assignments	I turned in a few class assignments	I didn't turn in any assignments		
Effort	I put forth a ton of effort	I put forth a lot of effort	I put forth some effort	I put forth little effort	I put forth no effort		
Progress							
Internet Searching	I learned or used a ton of new skills	I learned or used a lot of new skills	I learned or used some new skills	I learned or used a few new skills	I didn't learn anything new		
Library Skills	I learned or used a ton of new skills	I learned or used a lot of new skills	I learned or used some new skills	I learned or used a few new skills	I didn't learn anything new		
Products							
HERO PRODUCT # 1	My focus is very clear and my info is totally organized	My focus is clear and my info is mostly organized	My focus is sort of clear and my info is somewhat organized	My focus is fuzzy and I have very little info	My focus is fuzzy and I have no new information		
	I gathered info from a ton of sources	I gathered info from a lot of sources	I gathered info from some sources	I gathered info from a few sources	I gathered info from one source		
	I totally transformed the info into my own ideas	I mostly transformed the info into my own ideas	I somewhat transformed the info into my own ideas	I sort of transformed the info into my own ideas	I copied the info straight from the source		
HERO AGENDA	I presented two clear focus areas, formats, and totally accurate sources	I presented two clear focus areas, formats, and mostly accurate sources	I presented two clear focus areas, formats, and some sources	I had some focus areas and no sources	I did not have an agenda		
					TOTAL SCORE		

FIGURE 1 Search-Steps Assessment

1. Log online
2. go to a search site
3. type in a few key words
4. press search!
5. click on a site that looks good
6. write down all information that looks good.
7. go back and try another site until done.
8. Sign off.
9.
10.

derstand what you're thinking." To save time, we also administered individual offline search simulations and took note of students' responses. Example: "Let's say your family is given an exotic pet such as a leopard and you need to get information on the Internet. Talk through all the steps you'd go through to get the information you need." Another way we assessed students' searching ability was to assign a scavenger hunt that required them to search the Internet for specific facts. Our pretest scavenger hunt required students to find answers to the following high-interest questions: (1) How many actors have played James Bond? (2) Which U.S. president got stuck in his bathtub? (3) Who codirected the movie "Shrek"? The first hunt required two keywords that could be drawn directly from the question <actors +"James Bond">; the second hunt required three keywords <president + stuck + bathtub>; and the third hunt required a substitution <directors + Shrek>. The scavenger hunt was also an excellent teaching tool, since the students learned essential criteria about keyword strategies when Karen reviewed the activity with the whole class afterward.

Because keyword selection is a lynchpin to successful Internet searching, we also conducted a keyword pretest (see Figure 2) that required students to identify strong or weak keywords and provide an explana-

FIGURE 2   Partial Keyword Assessment

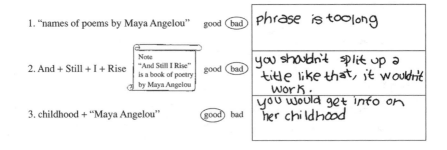

tion. This assessment was repeated throughout the unit (with comparable questions) in order to monitor student progress. As with the scavenger hunt, the keyword assessment was a powerful teaching tool when reviewed with the whole class afterward. It was surprising how weak the eighth graders in our study were at selecting appropriate keywords for their hero inquiries, even after instruction and practice. For example, we saw queries such as: <Mia + Hamm + Who influenced Mia to become a great soccer player>; <paul McCartney + become a Beatle>; <who were they + lucille balls parents>; <Poem + Leader of his country>; and <Red Sox + Nomar + Money he makes a year>. For more guidance on efficient keyword selection, see Eagleton and Guinee (2002).

Upon reflection, we would have included a questionnaire that assessed students' knowledge of computers and the Internet so that tech-savvy students could be enlisted for technical support for students who lacked computer skills. We also would have added a pre- and posttest that required students to identify appropriate research questions as, for example, too broad, appropriately focused, or too narrow.

While students were working on the pretests (we conducted one per day so as not to overwhelm students), Karen introduced search engines, gave a library tour, showed past student projects, and began exploring the hero theme with the class. Following a class discussion that defined a hero as, for example, real, researchable, and a role model, the students interviewed two adults and one student about heroes in various domains—artists, business leaders, earth keepers, explorers, humanitarians, scientists, athletes, and writers—in order to brainstorm possible topics for their research.

FIGURE 3   Subject-Knowledge Bubble Map

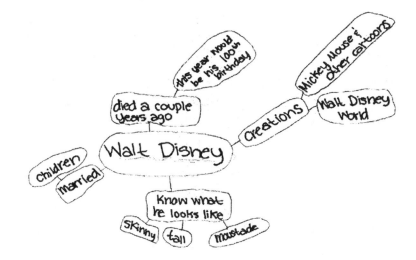

WEEK 2: KEYWORD INSTRUCTION

Although many students were eager to begin searching for information about a hero immediately, the second week of the project provided intensive instruction and practice in selecting keywords. Karen also modeled the inquiry process, emphasizing appropriate breadth and depth of topics and research questions; while it is tempting to focus on content acquisition or the final products of online research, it is imperative that language arts teachers emphasize the nature of the inquiry process instead. Once students selected their heroes, Karen assessed their prior subject knowledge before they began searching for information. In addition, students engaged in two more scavenger hunts and reviewed them afterward in order to facilitate practice and reinforcement of efficient keyword strategies.

A simple way to assess students' prior knowledge about their chosen hero was to ask them to draw a subject-knowledge bubble map (see Figure 3). This was a useful starting point for the students' inquiry, and also alerted Karen when students knew too much or too little about their topics to be successful. As with the other pretest measures, the subject-knowledge bubble map was repeated at the end of the project to measure student progress.

FIGURE 4   Keyword-Category Concept Map

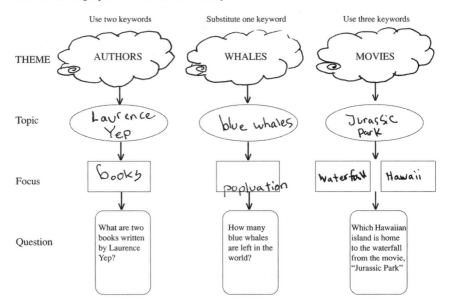

Fill in the missing topic and focus bubbles to find your search terms.

During the scavenger hunts, the primary tool we used for scaffolding students' understanding of keywords was the keyword-category concept map (see Figure 4), which required students to insert keywords into teacher-prepared templates with blank bubbles for topic and focus area. The topic and focus area then became the keywords. In the example above, the student began his scavenger hunt searches with <Laurence Yep + books>, <blue whales + population>, and <Jurassic Park + waterfall + Hawaii>.

The keyword-category concept maps were used for independent as well as guided practice in which the whole group worked with Karen to brainstorm topics and focus areas for each research question before actually searching the Internet for an answer. Students practiced identifying keywords that were directly stated in the question, keywords that needed to be substituted from the question, and searches that required more than two keywords.

FIGURE 5   Blank Web (L) and Completed Hero Project Map

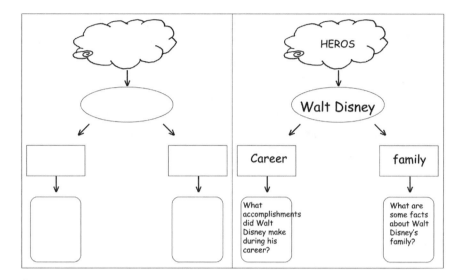

WEEK 3: NARROWING TOPICS

Week 3 was devoted to selecting focus areas, conferencing with the teacher, and beginning to search. It was a good time to address topic, audience, and purpose (TAP) for their final presentations, and to direct students' attention to the difference between a scavenger hunt, in which the search is for one fact that can be found on one website, and a research project, in which the search involves synthesizing and transforming complex information from multiple sources.

Since it is unrealistic to research everything about a hero in just a few weeks, students selected two areas on which to focus their inquiries, for example, family life, childhood, career, achievements, or personality. Our eighth graders brainstormed as many questions about their hero as they could and wrote them on notecards. Then they sorted the notecards into piles, based on the focus or content area of each question. Finally, they identified two areas of primary interest. A blank keyword-category concept map (see Figure 5) was helpful for identifying initial keywords for the students' selected focus areas. The student then used the keyword-category map to isolate <Walt Disney + career> and <Walt Disney + family> as appropriate keywords for starting her Internet research.

In preparation for conferencing with Karen, the students in our study carried out minisearches on their hero, and then prepared a rough draft of an agenda that they eventually revised and distributed to the class when presenting their research. On the agenda, the students identified two formats that appropriately matched their focus areas—a slide show on the hero's family life and a timeline of her/his achievements. They also stated why this person was their hero and identified at least three print resources and three websites that were potential resources for their inquiry. Once their hero was approved as worthwhile and researchable, the students were free to begin researching.

WEEK 4: SEARCHING

During the fourth week of the unit, students engaged in concentrated searching, both on the Internet and in the library. Karen's role was to observe closely and assist where needed, particularly with topic narrowing, research questions, and keyword selection, since these were the primary instructional objectives of the project. However, students also needed help analyzing search engine results, evaluating website relevancy and credibility, and documenting sources. In addition, we found note-taking and synthesizing to be particularly difficult for students of middle school age, so Karen provided guidance with those tasks as well.

When students felt they had collected enough information, they submitted their notes to Karen for review in order to confirm and ensure progress. At this time, students began collecting images and other artifacts to use in their final formats. Occasionally, students had to select a new hero because they were unable to find adequate information; in these cases, they submitted new subject knowledge bubble maps, focus area selections, and draft agendas before having a second conference.

WEEK 5: CONSTRUCTION

When Karen agreed that students had gathered sufficient information, the students began constructing their final formats. She helped them envision ways to transform the information they had collected into something original, another challenging task for this age group. Karen also reinforced appropriate matches between the focus area and the format used to present what had been learned. The expectations for various formats often needed clarification; for example, pasting magazine pictures on a poster without captions or any obvious organizational scheme did not demonstrate that learning had taken place. Multimedia productions that contained "bells and whistles" but lacked substantive content were other common pitfalls. Furthermore, although we expected middle-school students to be aware of the issue of plagiarism and be able to avoid it, many students copied and pasted entire websites in their final formats. Once formats were finalized, students submitted a final agenda with proper bibliographic documentation and prepared to present what they had learned.

In hindsight, we wish there had been time for Karen and/or peers to review rough drafts of the formats to ensure synthesis of content matter and demonstration of knowledge. Tricia Armstrong's excellent book, *Information Transformation: Teaching Strategies for Authentic Research, Projects, and Activities,* offers additional practical ideas.

WEEK 6: PRESENTING

The final week of the project was filled with posttests and student presentations. We found it wise to have students practice their presentations ahead of time, particularly those in digital formats that had to be preloaded. Students were asked to introduce their hero with relevant background information, present both formats, and conclude with a statement about why that person was their hero. Despite these instructions, it was surprising how many eighth graders failed to provide adequate background information about their heroes before presenting. As Karen notes:

> A student presented this morning on Jackie Robinson. She had a fabulous Inspiration [graphics program] document, which was a bubble map that she used to talk about his family. She had a PowerPoint that traced his career, and she had a fabulous skit in two scenes, which showed Jackie Robinson being turned away from a restaurant because

of his color. However, in the introduction, she didn't tell the class he was the first African American baseball player or that this happened before the Civil Rights Act in 1964, so he encountered a lot of discrimination. I knew that, but without that prior knowledge, the students had to kind of figure that out as they went through the presentation. So a lot of the impact of her information was lost.

Once students presented their work, they assessed themselves using the grading rubric and submitted it, along with their two formats, for final evaluation.

CONCLUSION

Searching the Internet for relevant information is a challenging literacy task for anyone, and is particularly difficult for middle-school students. It involves choosing topics, setting goals, asking questions, applying search strategies, selecting keywords, analyzing search results, evaluating website relevancy, documenting sources, note-taking, synthesizing, transforming, and presenting findings. Fortunately, most students are motivated to learn how to search the Internet more efficiently because they view computers as essential tools for communication and research (Eagleton, 2002).

Most of our students enjoyed the activities presented in this article because they focused on strengthening skills for online research. The hero theme was successful because students were allowed to research a self-selected topic of personal interest. Inquiry-based learning, such as this hero inquiry project, enables teachers to meet multiple instructional objectives and literacy standards while also integrating technology into the curriculum.

REFERENCES

Armstrong, T. (2000). *Information transformation: Teaching strategies for authentic research, projects, and activities.* Markham, Ontario: Pembroke.

Dutton, G. (2001, April). *Wising up the Web* (IT Forecaster Document #itf20010403). Framingham, MA: International Data.

Eagleton, M. B. (2002). Making text come to life on the computer: Toward an understanding of hypermedia literacy. *Reading Online,* 6(1). Retrieved April, 2006, from http://www.readingonline.org/articles/eagleton2/index.html

Eagleton, M. B., & Guinee, K. (2002). Strategies for supporting student Internet inquiry. *New England Reading Association Journal, 38*(2).

Leu, D. J., Jr. (2000). Our children's future: Changing the focus of literacy and literacy instruction. *Reading Teacher, 53,* 424–431.

National Center for Education Statistics. (2002). *Internet access in U.S. public schools and classrooms: 1994–2001.* Retrieved April, 2006, from http://nces.ed.gov/pub-search/pubsinfo.asp?pubid=2002018

NCTE/IRA. (1996). *Standards for the English language arts.* Urbana, IL: National Council of Teachers of English.

Rose, D. H., & Meyer, A. (2002). *Teaching every student in the digital age: Universal design for learning.* Alexandria, VA: ASCD.

Contributors

Peggy Coyne is an expert in the development of educational models that use technology. A research scientist at CAST, Dr. Coyne is a director of the Literacy by Design project, a three-year federally funded study using technology to improve literacy instruction for children with cognitive disabilities. As director of CAST's Family and Community Literacy Project in the 1990s, Dr. Coyne developed an innovative, technology-based model for supporting literacy development in at-risk families, and led the program's demonstration in schools, educational and social service organizations, libraries, and technology centers throughout the country. She holds her doctorate in education from Boston University.

Bridget Dalton is Chief Officer of Literacy and Technology at CAST. Her research focuses on the use of digital learning environments to support literacy learning and instruction for diverse learners. Dr. Dalton is currently coprincipal investigator, with Dr. Annemarie Palincsar, of a study of urban fourth-grade students' comprehension of informational text in a computer-based learning environment with embedded supports. That work is supported by the U.S. Department of Education's Institute for Educational Sciences. Previously, she was coeditor, with Dana Grisham of San Diego State University, of the International Reading Association's peer-reviewed electronic journal, *Reading Online*. Before joining CAST in 2000, Dr. Dalton was an associate professor at the University of Guam, where she chaired the graduate program in education, directed the College of Education's Literacy Center, and was editor of the journal *Micronesian Educator*. She earned her doctorate in reading, language, and learning disabilities at the Harvard Graduate School of Education.

Robert P. Dolan is a senior research scientist at CAST. Dr. Dolan provides leadership in the development of new methods and technologies for the assessment of learning that go beyond traditional outcome measures and better support Universal Design for Learning. Dr. Dolan brings expertise in visual and cognitive neuroscience and in user interface design and implementation to his educational research. He is coprincipal investigator in projects funded by the National Science Foundation and the U.S. Department of Education to explore new learning environments. In addition, with funding from a private foundation, Dr. Dolan directs a multiyear study of computer-based testing accommodations in large-scale assessments for students with learning disabilities. Dr. Dolan holds a PhD in brain and cognitive sciences from the Massachusetts Institute of Technology and a BS in biology from Cornell University.

Maya B. Eagleton is an adjunct assistant professor in language, reading, and culture at the University of Arizona's College of Education. She teaches courses in traditional literacies, electronic literacies, and qualitative research methods. Dr. Eagleton worked as a senior research scientist for CAST, where she researched and designed literacy software prototypes for students with learning disabilities. In particular, she conducted a major three-year research study funded by the U.S. Department of Education entitled "Trekking the Web: Internet Inquiry in a Supported Learning Environment for Students with Learning Disabilities." Dr. Eagleton has also served as a Title I coordinator, a Reading Recovery teacher, and an educational technology consultant. She is coauthor (with B. Dobler) of *Reading the Web: Teaching Strategies for Internet Inquiry* (in press, Guilford), an innovative, practical teacher handbook and college textbook that applies and extends research in print-based reading strategies to the complex process of reading and comprehending informational text on the Web.

Patricia Ganley manages CAST's school-based implementation of research and development projects, including teacher training, and classroom instruction and data collection. She also collaborates with teachers, programmers, researchers, and students to develop technological solutions for these projects, bringing to this work more than two decades of experience in education and psychology. Ms. Ganley serves on the advisory board for the Vermont-based Community Digital Storytelling Project, a K–16 collaborative effort to apply educational technology to a student-centered, community-based project. She holds a master's degree in education from Antioch University.

David Gordon is director of publishing and communications at CAST. Prior to joining CAST in 2004, he edited the *Harvard Education Letter*. He won a National Press Club award for distinguished reporting and analysis. The editor of three books, Mr. Gordon was a writer and reporter at *Newsweek* for several years and taught writing at Emerson College. He earned a BA with high honors from Columbia University, where he was elected to Phi Beta Kappa, and an MFA from Emerson College.

Kathleen Guinee is a doctoral candidate in human development and psychology at the Harvard Graduate School of Education. Her dissertation research examines factors that influence middle school students' efficiency and success during Web-based research. Ms. Guinee was a research assistant at CAST, where she worked on the Trekking the Web project with Dr. Maya Eagleton. She has been a visiting lecturer in assistive technologies and learning disabilities at Simmons College in Boston. Ms. Guinee has a bachelor of arts in computer science from Princeton University and holds a master's degree in education from the Mind, Brain, and Education program at Harvard.

Tracey Hall is a senior research scientist at CAST, where she specializes in alternative assessment and instructional design grounded in effective teaching practices. Dr. Hall has more than two decades of experience in curriculum-based measurement, teacher professional development, special-needs instruction, and curriculum development, project monitoring, and large-scale assessments. She directs CAST's initiatives to create and evaluate digital supported writing environments across content areas. Dr. Hall also has served as director of curriculum for the National Center on Accessing the General Curriculum (1999–2004), led by CAST. Before joining CAST, Dr. Hall was an assistant professor at Pennsylvania State University. She has been a special education teacher and administrator in public schools in Oregon. Dr. Hall received her PhD in special education from the University of Oregon.

Lani Harac is managing editor of *PTO Today*, a bimonthly magazine for leaders of K–8 parent-teacher organizations. She was previously an assistant editor at *Teacher Magazine*, and is an experienced newspaper journalist. In 2002, Ms. Harac was named Outstanding New Journalist by the Maryland Society of Professional Journalists. She holds degrees from the University of Florida and the University of North Carolina–Chapel Hill.

Kirsten Lee Howard currently teaches first grade in Springfield, Virginia. She has served as a kindergarten and special education teacher in both Boston, MA, and Virginia. She is dedicated to socially responsive curriculum that meets the needs of all students. Ms. Howard has presented workshops on conflict resolution, as well as ways of integrating technology into the curriculum to meet the needs of all students.

Karen Langlais teaches English at Ipswich Middle School in Ipswich, Massachusetts, where she serves on the districtwide curriculum development committee for English language arts. Karen received her undergraduate degree from Simmons College and her master's from Salem State College.

Grace Meo manages professional development programs and outreach services for CAST, which she helped to cofound in 1984. She oversees a national network of school practitioners that collaborate with CAST on researching, designing, modeling, and disseminating universally designed materials and practices that address the needs of all learners. Ms. Meo has served as director of research-to-practice for the National Center on Accessing the General Curriculum, leading state-level initiatives to train teachers in the use of universally designed curricula and instructional approaches. Ms. Meo holds a master's degree in early childhood education from the Boston College Graduate School of Education, and a BA in psychology from Regis College.

Anne Meyer is a founding director of CAST, where she is also its chief officer of educational design. Dr. Meyer has also led efforts to refine and disseminate CAST's ideas about Universal Design for Learning through writing and website development. Anne Meyer is a coauthor (with David Rose) of two books, the seminal *Teaching Every Student in the Digital Age: Universal Design for Learning* (ASCD, 2002) and *Learning to Read in the Computer Age* (Brookline Books, 1998), as well as numerous journal articles. Dr. Meyer is also coeditor, with David Rose and Chuck Hitchcock, of *The Universally Designed Classroom: Accessible Curriculum and Digital Technologies* (Harvard Education Press, 2005). Widely recognized for her contributions in the field of technology as it relates to disabilities, Dr. Meyer was a national advisor to President Clinton's Educational Technology Panel and a 1995 recipient of a Gold Medal from the National Association of Social Sciences. Dr. Meyer completed her undergraduate work at Radcliffe College and received her master's and doctoral degrees from the Harvard Graduate School of Education. She is a licensed clinical psychologist.

Elizabeth Murray is a senior research scientist and instructional designer at CAST, where she applies her technical skills, mathematics background, special education experience, and clinical specialties to the development of universally designed software. Dr. Murray is coprincipal investigator for the U.S. Department of Education's Steppingstones of Technology Innovation program, "Thinking Writer for Science: A Technology-Based Approach for Writing to Support Students with Disabilities." She has also served as coprincipal investigator for a federally funded project to develop and test a prototype of a digital high school biology text containing embedded supports for student learning, in collaboration with the Center for Research on Learning at the University of Kansas. Before joining CAST, Dr. Murray was an assistant professor in the Department of Occupational Therapy at Sargent College of Health and Rehabilitation Sciences, where she had earned a Doctor of Science degree from Boston

University. Her doctoral research analyzed the relationship between visual-spatial abilities and mathematics achievement in boys with and without learning disabilities. She has also been an elementary and special education teacher in the Philadelphia Public Schools.

Bart Pisha served as a principal investigator or project director for a number of federally funded projects at CAST focused on developing technology-based instructional approaches for students with learning disabilities. He received his master's degree from Goddard College and his doctorate from the Harvard Graduate School of Education. Before joining CAST in 1993, he taught in public elementary schools and at the undergraduate and graduate levels. He has held teaching fellowships in reading instruction, research methodology, and statistics at Harvard. Dr. Pisha, who has a documented learning disability, is a member of the Board of Directors of the International Dyslexia Association.

David H. Rose helped to found CAST in 1984 with a vision of expanding opportunities for all students, especially those with disabilities, through the innovative development and application of new technologies. Dr. Rose lectures at the Harvard Graduate School of Education, where he has been on the faculty for twenty years. He has been the lead researcher on a number of U.S. Department of Education grants, and is currently the principal investigator of two national centers created to develop and implement the National Instructional Materials Accessibility Standard. He is a coauthor of highly successful educational software such as Literary Place, WiggleWorks, and Thinking Reader. Dr. Rose is the coauthor with Anne Meyer of the books *Teaching Every Student in the Digital Age: Universal Design for Learning* (ASCD, 2002) and *Learning to Read in the Computer Age* (Brookline, 1998), and the author of numerous articles. Dr. Rose is also coeditor, with Anne Meyer and Chuck Hitchcock, of *The Universally Designed Classroom: Accessible Curriculum and Digital Technologies* (Harvard Education Press, 2005). He is a frequent speaker at regional and national educational conferences. Dr. Rose holds a BA in psychology from Harvard College, a master's degree in teaching from Reed College, and a doctorate in education from the Harvard Graduate School of Education. In 2004, he was named one of education's "Daring Dozen" by the George Lucas Educational Foundation's *Edutopia* magazine.

Skip Stahl is CAST's director of technical assistance and is project director for the National Instructional Materials Accessibility Standard (NIMAS) Development Center, a cooperative agreement with the U.S. Department of Education, Office of Special Education Programs. Mr. Stahl chaired the National File Format Technical Panel for the department, building consensus among diverse stakeholders to write the first version of NIMAS. A nationally recognized expert in Universal Design for Learning, Mr. Stahl has extensive experience in providing professional development and assistance to educators in K–12 and postsecondary settings. He received a BA in English literature from Bard College and an MS from Bank Street College of Education.

Nicole Strangman is a writer and editor at CAST, where she contributes to journal articles, reports, and book chapters, and provides research services. Dr. Strangman brings to her writing responsibilities at CAST a strong background in basic scientific research. She holds a BA in biology from Swarthmore College and a PhD in neuroscience from Brown University. As a researcher, Dr. Strangman has special expertise in the pharmacology of chronic pain, spinal cord electrophysiology, and immunohistochemistry, and has published numerous refereed and invited articles in scholarly publications.

Index

REPRINTED WITH PERMISSION

"Frequent Questions about Universal Design for Learning" by Grace Meo originally appeared as "Curriculum Access for All" in the *Harvard Education Letter* (November/December 2005, pp. 4–6). Reprinted with permission of the publisher.

"A Level Playing Field: UDL in the Classroom" by Lani Harac originally appeared as "A Level Playing Field" in *Teacher Magazine* (October 2004, vol 16, no. 2, pp. 40–45). Copyright 2004, Editorial Projects in Education. All rights reserved. Reprinted with permission of the publisher.

"Teacher Perspectives: UDL in the Elementary Classroom" by Kirsten Lee Howard originally appeared in *Learning and Leading with Technology* (February 2004, vol. 31, no. 5). Copyright 2004, Kirsten Lee Howard. Reprinted with permission of the author.

"Teacher Perspectives: Strategy Instruction Goes Digital" by Nicole Strangman originally appeared as "Strategy Instruction Goes Digital: Two Teachers' Perspectives on Digital Texts with Embedded Learning Supports" in *Reading Online* (2003, vol. 6, no. 9). Reprinted with permission of the International Reading Association.

"Implications of Universal Design for Learning for Classroom Assessment" by David H. Rose and Robert P. Dolan originally appeared as "Universal Design for Learning: Assessment" in the online *Journal of Special Education Technology* (Fall 2000, vol. 5, no. 4).

"Engaging the Text: Brain Research and the Universal Design of Reading Strategy Supports" by David H. Rose and Bridget Dalton originally appeared as "Using Technology to Individualize Reading Instruction" in C. C. Block, L. B. Gambrell, and M. Pressley (Eds.), *Improving Comprehension Instruction: Rethinking Research, Theory, and Classroom Practice* (San Francisco: Jossey-Bass, 2002). Reprinted with permission and edited for this volume.

"Teaching Internet Literacy Strategies: The Hero Inquiry Project" by Maya B. Eagleton, Kathleen Guinee, and Karen Langlais originally appeared in *Voices from the Middle* (March 2003, vol. 10, no. 3). Reprinted with permission of the National Council of Teachers of English.